Adoption-centric Usability Engineering

T0255079

Ahmed Seffah · Eduard Metzker

Adoption-centric Usability Engineering

Systematic Deployment, Assessment
and Improvement of Usability Methods
in Software Engineering

 Springer

Ahmed Seffah, PhD
Department of Computer Science
   and software Engineering
Concordia University, Montreal, Canada

Eduard Metzker, PhD
Software Technology Research Centre
DaimlerChrysler, Ulm, Germany

ISBN: 978-1-84996-703-7   e-ISBN: 978-1-84800-019-3
DOI 10.1007/978-1-84800-019-3

British Library Cataloguing in Publication Data
A catalogue record for this book is available from the British Library

© Springer-Verlag London Limited 2010
Apart from any fair dealing for the purposes of research or private study, or criticism or review, as
permitted under the Copyright, Designs and Patents Act 1988, this publication may only be reproduced,
stored or transmitted, in any form or by any means, with the prior permission in writing of the
publishers, or in the case of reprographic reproduction in accordance with the terms of licences issued
by the Copyright Licensing Agency. Enquiries concerning reproduction outside those terms should be
sent to the publishers.
The use of registered names, trademarks, etc., in this publication does not imply, even in the absence of a
specific statement, that such names are exempt from the relevant laws and regulations and therefore free
for general use.
The publisher makes no representation, express or implied, with regard to the accuracy of the
information contained in this book and cannot accept any legal responsibility or liability for any errors
or omissions that may be made.

Printed on acid-free paper

Springer Science+Business Media
springer.com

For my wife Malika
For my gazelles Assia and Rania
For Simane le Grand and Idriss
  Boutchou

Contents

List of Figures

List of Tables

Executive Summary

Developing software systems which are easy to use while simultaneously increasing the productivity, performance and satisfaction of users is still a major challenge in software engineering. Thus a large number of usability engineering methods have been proposed to systematically develop software with high usability. A large number of studies indicate that even basic usability engineering methods are not integrated in software development lifecycles practiced in industrial settings. Yet problems in the adoption of methods by project teams are rarely examined.

This book provides a new perspective on the integration and adoption of usability engineering methods by software development teams. The adoption of methods by project teams – contrary to popular belief – is not assured just because it is mandated by the organization. This work argues that usability engineering methods can only be regarded as integrated in the software development process of an organization when these methods are practiced and accepted by development teams. So far no frameworks for examining the acceptance of methods by project teams and for exploiting such data for guiding project teams in method deployment are available.

To address this problem, this book presents an approach which consists of a process meta-model for guiding project teams in the deployment of usability engineering methods and a measurement framework for measuring the acceptance of the deployed methods. The approach is called Adoption-Centric Usability Engineering. The approach provides a concept to capture usability engineering methods together with a context profile. The context profile encodes the factors which contributed to the acceptance or rejection of the respective methods in past projects. This context-sensitive description of a usability engineering method introduced in this work is called a USEPack (Usability Engineering Experience Package).

For guiding project teams in integrating usability engineering methods into their development processes the approach developed in this work introduces the concept of a usability engineering method kit. A usability engineering method kit is an abstraction of a usability engineering methodology which separates process phases and activities from the specific methods to perform them. The assignment of methods to certain activities is not predefined. They are chosen to best fit the characteristics of a project at hand. Usability engineering methods are linked to a usability engineering method kit in the form of USEPacks. The linking of USEPacks to a method kit is based on the characteristics of the project in which the method kit is to be deployed and on the acceptance rating which the USEPacks received in previous projects.

To measure the acceptance of each USEPack after deployment, the approach proposes to use existing theories of technology acceptance. Based on these theories the perceived usefulness and ease-of-use of each USEPack deployed in a project is assessed by the project team to measure the acceptance of the USEPack.

The approach provides concepts which exploit the collected data to adapt the context profiles of the deployed USEPacks. After a number of iterations the context profiles of USEPacks reflect the factors which contributed to the acceptance or rejection of a USEPack by project teams. This knowledge can be used in future projects to guide the selection of appropriate methods and to improve the acceptance of usability engineering methods by project teams.

The concepts of the Adoption-Centric Usability Engineering approach are implemented in a supporting Web-based system. The system, called ProUSE, allows project teams to configure project specific method kits and assess the acceptance of the deployed USEPacks as well as to build and maintain the pool of USEPacks. ProUSE fuses and exploits the data gathered in the acceptance assessments to optimize the project specific selection of appropriate usability engineering methods.

An evaluation of the developed framework with potential users of the Adoption-Centric Usability Engineering approach is performed. Forty four project team members of five software development organizations participated in the evaluation. The evaluation shows that project team members understand the objectives of the approach and can transfer the concepts to their processes. Moreover the evaluation shows that the approach as it is embodied in the support environment ProUSE is perceived as useful and easy to use by project teams. The evaluation indicates that the Adoption-Centric Usability Engineering approach has the potential to improve the introduction and establishment of usability engineering methods in software development processes.

Target Audience

The main target audience of this book is software developers, managers, and educators from both academia and industry. It provides them with a complete, comprehensive, step-by-step approach for integrating usability in the software development lifecycle. The book is also designed to be useful for usability and educators specialists who are interested in the development of methodologies and standards, who have researched or developed specific usability techniques, or who have worked with software development methodologies. It also offers insights on how to integrate usability techniques and tools with software engineering methodologies. The book can support any person interested in the general problem of promoting usability in the software development community. Software developers and educators can use it to extend and improve their methodologies, and to learn techniques for communicating with usability specialists and supporters. The book introduces User-Centered Design (UCD) techniques as compliments to the existing software development strategies rather than as a replacement.

Part I
Usability Engineering: Definitions, Methods, and Challenges for Integration

Chapter 1
On Usability and Usability Engineering

Several cost–benefits studies demonstrated the importance of usability while highlighting the current gap between usability and software engineering methods and tools. In this introductory chapter we outline the importance of usability as a software quality attribute as well as the importance and fundamentals of its engineering and integration into the mainstream software development lifecycle.

1.1 Interactive Systems and User Interface

Recent years have seen the emergence of a wide variety of new computing hardware. In addition to traditional desktop graphical user interface (GUI) style applications, the variety of interactive systems exhibiting new interaction styles includes: interactive televisions controlled by hand-held remotes, Internet-enabled televisions (WebTVs), mobile phones with small screens and keypads, Personal Digital Assistants (PDAs) with pen-based input, smart whiteboards and virtual reality applications where users interact with the contents using sensor-based devices.

Software architecture is a fundamental design organization of a system, embodied in its components, their relationships to each other, and the principles governing its design, development and evolution (ANSI/IEEE 1471-2000, Recommended Practice for Architectural Description of Software-Intensive Systems). In addition, it encapsulates the fundamental entities and properties of the application that generally ensure the quality of application including reliability, robustness and reusability. However, usability, which is more and more recognized as being an important quality factor has been neglected in these architectural models (e.g. see ISO 9126 on software quality metrics).

In the field of human–computer interaction, interactive systems architectures of the 1980s and 1990s such as MVC (Model, View, Controller) and PAC (Presentation, Abstraction and Control) are based on the principle of separating the core functionality from the user interface. The functionality is what the software actually does and what data it processes, thereby offering behavior that can be exploited to achieve some user needs. The user interface defines how the functionality is presented to end-users and how the users interact with it.

A. Seffah, E. Metzker, *Adoption-centric Usability Engineering*,
DOI 10.1007/978-1-84800-019-3_1, © Springer-Verlag London Limited 2009

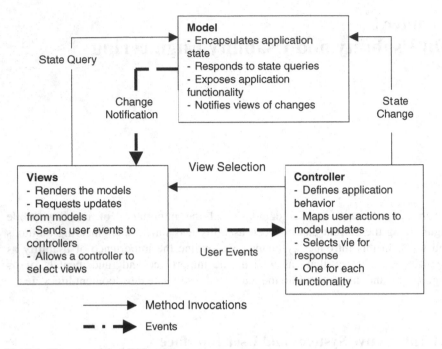

Fig. 1.1 The roles of the MVC architecture components

The following are the three main components (Fig. 1.1):

- Abstraction or model which contains the functionality of the software. A model can have several views. When a user manipulates a view of a model, the view informs a controller of the desired change.
- Control or dialog.
- Presentation, which provides GUI components for a model. It gets the values that it displays by querying the model of which it is a view.

The controller can take many forms, but it is always responsible for the five following services to the users:

- Dialog (User–computer Interaction)
- Errors and feedback
- Help and support
- Information presentation and visualization
- Input and output devices

The motivation behind this architectural model and similar ones is to improve, among others, the adaptability, portability, complexity handling and separation of concerns of interactive software. However, even if the principle of separating interactive software into components has its design merits, it can be a source of serious adaptability and usability problems in software that provides fast, frequent and intensive semantic feedback. The communication between the view and the model makes the software system highly coupled and complex.

The underlying assumption is that usability, the ultimate quality factor, is primarily a property of the user interface. Therefore separating the user interface from the application's logic makes it easy to modify, adapt or customize the interface after user testing. Unfortunately, this assumption does not ensure the usability of the system as a whole. For example, Len Bass and his colleagues (Bass et al., 2003) identified specific connections between aspects of usability (such as the ability to "undo") and the model response (processed by an event-handler routine).

We now realize that system features can have an impact on the usability of the system, even if they are logically independent from the user interface and not necessarily visible to the user. For example, Bass et al. observed that even if the presentation of a system is well designed, the usability of a system can be greatly compromised if the underlying architecture and designs do not have the proper provisions for user concerns. Software architecture should define not only the technical issues needed to develop and implement the functionality, but also dialogs with the users.

At the core of our vision is that invisible components that are the implementations of the functionality can affect usability. By invisible components, we mean precisely any software entity or architectural attribute that does not have visible cues on the presentation layer. They can be an operation, data, or a structural attribute of the software. Examples of such phenomena where invisible components affect usability are commonplace in database modeling. Queries that were not anticipated by the modeler, or that turn out to be more frequent than expected, can take forever to complete because the logical data model (or even the physical data model) is inappropriate. Client-server and distributed computer architectures are also particularly prone to usability problems stemming from their "invisible" components.

Another example came from the Web where designers of distributed applications with Web browser-based user interfaces are often faced with these concerns. They must carefully weigh what part of the application logic will reside on the client side and what part will be on the server side in order to achieve an appropriate level of usability. User feedback information, such as application status and error messages, must be carefully designed and exchanged between the client and server part of the application, anticipating response time of each component, error conditions and exception handling, and the variability of the computing environment. Sometimes, the Web user interface becomes crippled by the constraints imposed by these invisible components because the appropriate and required style of interactions is too difficult to implement.

Like other authors (Bass and John, 2003), we argue that both software developers implementing the system's features and usability engineers in charge of designing the user interfaces should be aware of the importance of this intimate relationship between the way that the features are implemented and the user interfaces. This relationship can inform architecture design for usability. As discussed in this paper, with the help of patterns that incorporate the attributes that quantify usability, this relationship can help to integrate usability concerns in software architecture while ensuring the usability of the product. We will identify scenarios where invisible components of an interactive application will impact on usability; we will also propose solutions to each scenario. The solutions are presented in the form of patterns. Beyond proposing a list of patterns to solve specific problems, we will detail a measurement-oriented framework for studying and integrating usability concerns in interactive software architecture via patterns and usability measures.

1.2 Usability: A Quality Attribute of the Whole System, Not Just the User Interface

Usability has been considered and perceived with a variety of meanings by different groups of people.

As teachers in Human–Computer Interaction (HCI), we are often surprised at how rarely computer-science students understand usability beyond the basic ease-of-use concept, and how these students have little idea of how to decompose or measure it.

As consultants in software engineering projects, we are also surprised at how usability is viewed as a "window dressing" discipline with a focus on style guides as the ultimate usability reference for the project.

For many software engineers, usability simply means "ease-of-use" or "user friendly", a term introduced in the early days of Human–Computer Interaction. We still find this term in many project requirements definitions, standing alone among other non-functional requirements, as though this expression encompasses all there is to know about the field.

The IEEE Std.610.12-1990 standard reflects this perception of usability: "The ease with which a user can learn to operate, to prepare inputs for, and to interpret outputs of a system or component".

In the HCI community, as a quality factor, the ISO 9241-11 (1998) standard defines usability as: "the extent to which a product can be used by a specified set of users to achieve specified goals (tasks) with effectiveness, efficiency and satisfaction in a certain context of use." The standard also states that the term *usability* is often used to refer to the capability of a product to be used easily.

This corresponds to the definition of usability as a software quality attribute in the ISO/IEC 9126 (2001) standard. This standard defines usability as: "a set of quality attributes that bear on the effort needed for use, and on the individual assessment of such use, by a stated or implied set of users." In its 1999 revision, this standard redefines usability as: "the capability of the software product to be understood learned, used and attractive to the user, when used under specified conditions."

In its latest revision, ISO/IEC 9126-1 provides a quality model for software products consisting of two parts: (a) external and internal quality, and (b) quality in use. It considers usability as a characteristic of external and internal quality that can be measured using the product's external and internal attributes.

ISO/IEC 9126-1 defines quality in use as: "the capability of the software product to enable specified users to achieve specified goals with effectiveness, productivity, safety and satisfaction in specified context of use."

Usability is generally defined in terms of relationships with a set of factors. The intimate cause and effect relationship that exists between usability and these factors makes usability very difficult to assess and measure. The factors are:

- Efficiency, the capability of the software product to enable users to expend an appropriate amount of resources in relation to the results achieved in a specified context of use
- Effectiveness, the capability of the software product to enable users to achieve specified goals with accuracy and completeness in a given context of use
- Satisfaction, users' subjective approval while using a software product in a specified context of use and
- Learnability, the ease with which users can master the required features for achieving their goals in a certain context of use

Some of these definitional attributes are summarized in Table 1.1. Each row in the table lists areas of apparent agreement concerning attributes of usability. For example, all sources in Table 1.1 describe "efficiency" as a usability attribute, although not all sources use this particular term (e.g., Nielsen, 1994b; Schneiderman, 1992). Also, not all sources in Table 1.1 include the same core set of usability attributes. Both characteristics just mentioned can be a source of confusion for researchers and developers alike. These examples highlight the need for a consolidated model about usability measurement with consistent terms for usability attributes and metrics.

Table 1.1 Usability attributes of various standards or models

Constantine and Lockwood (1999)	ISO 9241-11 (1998)	Schneiderman (1992)	Nielsen (1994)	Preece et al. (1994)	Shackel (1991)
Efficiency in use	Efficiency	Speed of performance	Efficiency of use	Throughput	Effectiveness (Speed)
Learnability		Time to learn	Learnability (Ease of learning)	Learnability (Ease of learning)	Learnability (Time to learn)
Rememberability		Retention over time	Memorability		Learnability (Retention)
Reliability in use		Rate of errors by users	Errors/safety	Throughput	Effectiveness (Errors)
User satisfaction	Satisfaction Comfort and acceptability of use)	Subjective satisfaction	Satisfaction	Attitude	Attitude

1.3 Usability in Traditional Software Quality Models

The idea of usability has been represented in various software engineering quality models for at least three decades. For example, McCall, Richards, and Walters (1977) described one of the earliest of these models referred to as the GE (General Electric) model or FCM (Factors, Criteria and Metrics) model. This hierarchical quality model was made up of a total of 11 quality factors, 25 quality criteria, and 41 specific quality metrics. In this model, quality factors are hypothetical constructs that correspond to the external view of the system as perceived by its users. A hypothetical construct as defined by Nunnally and Bernstein (1994) reflects the hypothesis that a variety of specific measures will correlate with one another or will be similarly affected by experimental manipulation. Hypothetical constructs, such as "software usability" and "software comprehension," are not directly measurable. Instead, they can be only inferred indirectly through observed measures, such as those for perceived effectiveness, user satisfaction and performance evaluation.

Usability in McCall's model is decomposed into three criteria: operability, training, and effectiveness. A quality criterion can be related to more than one factor and is directly measurable with specific metrics. Similar to McCall model, Boehm (1988) quality model is also hierarchical. It assumes that quality attributes are higher-order characteristics (hypothetical constructs) that are not directly measurable. Also similar to McCall's model, quality attributes (factors) are decomposed into quality criteria, which in turn are decomposed into directly measurable characteristics (metrics). Boehm's model incorporates 19 different quality factors encompassing product utility, maintainability, and portability. However, specific metrics in Boehm's model are not always associated with the same quality factors as in McCall's models, which can cause confusion.

1.4 Other Specific Measurement Models

Besides the standards and models proposed by traditional software engineering approaches, some other models and tools for evaluating usability have been proposed over the last 15 years. Some of the most influential works in this area are described next.

The Metrics for Usability Standards in Computing (MUSiC; Bevan, 2000; Macleod et al., 1997) model was concerned specifically with defining measures of software usability, many of which were integrated into the original ISO 9241 standard. Examples of specific usability metrics in the MUSiC framework include user performance measures, such as task effectiveness, temporal efficiency, and length or proportion of productive period. However, a strictly performance-based view of usability cannot reflect other aspects of usability, such as user satisfaction or learnability. As part of the MUSiC project, a 50-item user satisfaction questionnaire called the Software Usability Measurement Inventory (SUMI; Kirakowski and Corbett, 1993) was developed to provide measures of global satisfaction and of five more specific usability areas, including effectiveness, efficiency, helpfulness, control, and learnability.

The Skill Acquisition Network (SANe; Macleod and Rengger, 1993) model dealt with the analysis of the quality of use of interactive devices. This approach assumes a user interaction model that defines user tasks, the dynamics of the device, and procedures for executing user tasks. Specifically, a task model and a device model are simultaneously developed and subsequently linked. Next, user procedures are simulated within the linked task-device model. A total of 60 different metrics are described in this framework, of which 24 concern quality measures. Scores from the latter are then combined to form a total of five composite quality measures, including:

- Efficiency, which is determined by the estimated costs (e.g., total time) of executing user procedures
- Learning, which is defined as the number of states and state transitions necessary to carry out user tasks
- Adaptiveness, which concerns the functionality of the device within a given application domain
- Cognitive workload, which is determined by the controllability of the application, decision complexity (alternatives from which the user can choose), and memory load
- Effort for error correction, which concerns the robustness of a device and the costs for error recovery

The semi-Automated Interface Designer and Evaluator (AIDE, Sears, 1995) model provided a software tool to evaluate static HyperText Markup Language (HTML) pages according to a set of predetermined guidelines about Web page design. These guidelines concern things such as the placement and alignment of screen elements (e.g., text, buttons, or links). The AIDE tool can also generate alternative interface layouts and evaluate some aspects of a design. Designs are evaluated in AIDE according to both task-sensitive metrics and task-independent metrics. Task-sensitive metrics incorporate task information into the development process, which may ensure that user tasks guide the semantics of interface design. Task-independent metrics tend to be based on principles of graphic design and help to ensure that the interface is aesthetically pleasing. Altogether the AIDE tool can measure a total of five different usability metrics, including efficiency, alignment, horizontal balance, vertical balance, and designer-specified constraints (e.g., element positioning).

The Diagnostic Recorder for Usability Measurement (DRUM; Macleod and Rengger, 1993) is a software tool for analyzing user-based evaluations and the delivery of these data to the appropriate party, such as a usability engineer. The Log Processor component of DRUM is the tool concerned with metrics. It calculates several different performance-based usability metrics, including:

- Task time, or the total time required for each task under study
- Snag, help, and search times, which concern the amount of time users spend dealing with problems such as seeking help or unproductively hunting through a system

- Effectiveness, which as a metric is derived from measures of the quantity and quality of task output and measures whether users succeed in achieving their goals when working with a system
- Efficiency, which relates effectiveness to the task time and thus measures the rate of task output
- Relative efficiency, which indicates how efficiently a task is performed by a general user compared with an expert user on the same system or with the same task on another system
- Productive period, or the proportion of task time *not* spent in snag, help, or search (i.e., the relative amount of productive work time)

The Goals, Operators, Methods, and Selection rules (GOMS; John and Kieras, 1996) model for a particular task consists of descriptions of the methods needed to accomplish specified goals with a software system. The methods are a series of steps consisting of operations that the user must perform with that system. A method may call for subgoals to be accomplished, so methods have a hierarchical structure in the GOMS framework. If more than one method is needed in order to accomplish a goal, then the model outlines selection rules that can be used to choose the appropriate method depending on the context. By adding estimated time to accomplish a task as part of the description of a task, the GOMS model can be used to predict aspects of the expert user performance, such as total task time. This predictive model can be useful during the task analysis phase, but a fully functional system is eventually needed to collect measurements that verify the predictions.

The National Institute of Standards and Technology (NIST) Web Metrics (Scholtz and Laskowski, 1998) is a set of six computer tools and several metrics that support rapid, remote, and automated testing and evaluation of website usability. In their study on empirically validated Web page design metrics, Melody and Hearst (2001) found that usability prediction with the help of metrics matches in some cases up to 80% of the results based on expert evaluation of the same Web pages.

1.5 Cost–benefits of Usability Engineering

A strong commitment to usability offers enormous benefits. Among the measurable effects of usability, one can mention decreasing the training costs and time, facilitating the transition to new versions of a system, ensuring better quality of work, and minimizing the risk of user errors in data entry. Usability can affect other areas including human productivity and performance, safety and commercial viability. Usability is important not only to increase the speed and accuracy of the range of tasks carried out by a range of users of a system, but also to ensure the safety of the user (prevention of Repetitive Strain Injury etc.). The success of commercial software may hinge on these reviews, just as the success of any software relies on the attitude of its users. Attitudes can be influenced by abstract factors such as the look and feel of a product, and how the software can be customized by the user (e.g. colors, fonts, and commands).

Table 1.2 Statistics for justifying the cost-benefits of usability

---

- 80% of software development costs occur after the product is released, in the maintenance phase.
- Of those costs, 80% are due to unmet or unseen user requirements.
- Only 20% of post-development costs are due to bugs or reliability problems.
- It is 40–100% more expensive to fix problems in the maintenance phase than in the design phase.
- Systems designed with usability principles in mind typically reduce the time needed for training by 25%.
- User-centered design typically cuts errors in user-system interaction by 1–5%.
- The American Express Customer Service Department observed the following consequences after improving the usability and learnability of their existing system: (1) reduced employee training, from 12 hours to 2 hours, (2) improved productivity, from 17 minutes to 4 minutes per request, (3) decreased data entry error rate, from 20% to 2%.
- If we consider that training might easily cost $100/hour and that American Express had to train 1000 employees, then the switch to the new more usable system saved the company $1 million in training alone!

One study found that an average of 48% of application code is devoted to the UI, and 50% of the development time required for the entire application is devoted to the UI (Myers, 1995). The most important justification for usability and Human-Centered Software Engineering (HCSE) research is that about 80% of software maintenance costs are the result of problems users have with what the system does, and have nothing to do with programming bugs (Boehm, 1991) and (Pressman, 1992) (see Table 1.2 for other justifications of usability). Landauer (1995) and Bevan (2000) also cite many studies regarding the benefits of usability engineering.

Most of the cost–benefits studies do not include all major aspects of usability and how they are related to the assumed benefits. Measures of usability are also not well integrated into current software engineering practices, and they often lack computer tool support, too. One consequence of these weaknesses is that perhaps most software developers do not apply correctly any particular model in the evaluation of usability. This is not surprising given that there are few clear guidelines about how various definitions of usability factors, rules, and criteria are related (if at all) and how to select or measure specific aspects of usability for particular computer applications. Instead, actual practice tends to be ad hoc such that usability professionals may assume some benefits with which they are familiar. The selection of any usability method may not be optimal in many cases. That is, the effort to measure the effect on applying a usability method may be wasted without a consistent and consolidated framework for measuring usability.

1.6 Involving the End-User is Central, but Not Enough

Like others, we argue that a substantial quantity of these post-release development costs are due to the fact that current Software Engineering (SE) methodologies do not apply sufficient attention to: (a) user needs and usability requirements, and

(b) testing and validating requirements, design prototypes and fully functional systems with end-users before the deployment of the system (before, during and after development).

Human-centric design and engineering approaches have emerged to compensate for these weaknesses of traditional engineering methods. As a process, HCSE is concerned with the planning, development and production of interactive software systems. HCSE pays specific attention to the needs of end-users and the ways in which products can be made safe, easy to use, and a comfortable fit with the way people live (Owen and Agerfalk, 2004). In our perception of human centric-design, usability should be considered throughout the overall product design and not just during User Interface (UI) design, as is the case today.

ISO Standard 13407 defines HCD (Human-Centered Design) as "the active involvement of users and a clear understanding of the user and their tasks; an appropriate allocation of function between users and technology; the iteration of design solutions which requires a multidisciplinary design team." It also states that users' needs, personalities and the way they interact with a system should dominate the system's whole design. Thus HCD requires knowledge about:

- The future users of the system: User profile, behavior, experiences, background and skill level, etc. - The kinds of tasks the users will be doing with the interactive system
- The work context and social environment in which the system will be used
- The required quality factors including technical and technological

The entire HCD approach is based on three major principles that should be at the core of any development process (Gould and Lewis, 1985):

1. An early focus on users, their tasks and the context in which the system will be used
2. Empirical measurement, where the system's usability is assessed via a set of guidelines and metrics
3. Iterative design, a cycle whereby design concepts are repeatedly proposed, evaluated, refined and tested. In design solution iteration, user feedback is a critical source of improvements

Figure 1.2 portrays the main differences between user-centered versus the traditional engineering approach which is functionality-oriented.

Despite strong evidence for why we should adopt the HCD approach and the associated usability engineering toolbox, a large percentage of projects still do not apply up-to-date HCD design methods. Even when HCD is considered, it is often not well integrated with SE practices, resulting in a weakened approach.

Usability engineering remains the province of visionaries, isolated departments, enlightened software practitioners and large organizations, rather than the everyday practice of the typical software developer. Knowledge and theory is still scarce about how to efficiently and smoothly incorporate UE (User Experience) methods into established software development processes.

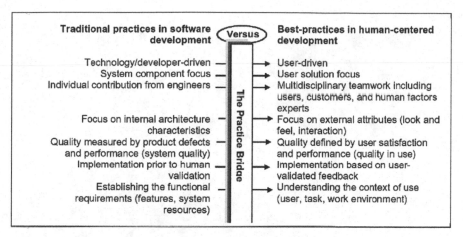

Fig. 1.2 Centered versus system-oriented development approaches

While standards such as ISO 13407 (Human-Centered Design Processes for Interactive Systems) provide means to assess an organization's capability to adopt HCD practices, they don't provide guidance on how to actually implement process improvement and organizational strategies that lead to an effective integration. Often, it remains unclear to software and UE professionals if, and why, certain UE tools and methods are better suited than others in a certain development context.

Moreover, HCD has been historically presented as the opposite, and sometimes as a replacement, to the functionality driven philosophy that we generally find behind the software engineering toolbox (Norman, 1998). The reality is that UE and software engineering techniques each have their own strengths and weaknesses and their objectives overlap in some areas but differ in others.

UE methods should be seen as a core part of every software development activity. Yet, despite their well-documented paybacks, they remain to be widely adopted. We argue that an integrated framework that incorporates design, development and evaluation principles from both fields will bring more effective use of UE within software development while helping HCI/UE community to develop a new generation of methods.

Chapter 2
Usability Engineering Methods Plethora

This chapter briefly surveys the broad range of usability engineering methods that have been proposed. It defines the major concepts and principles of usability methods, and contrasts the differences between usability engineering techniques, methods-sensitive to usability and traditional software methods. Although it is not an exhaustive account of all the current methods, the chapter describes a subset of well-established and widely practiced methods that can be successfully applied in industry.

Most of the methods included in this chapter are applicable to a wide range of systems and as such can be used to obtain design feedback, metrics and subjective data regardless of the particular application domain. Many of the methods can also be used to study different user groups, such as novices and experts. The methods selected for inclusion represent established approaches, which have been successfully applied in industry. A short list of other methods of potential value is also included in this chapter. This extra list includes UCD-sensitive processes as well as extensions to traditional software engineering methodologies and lifecycles.

2.1 Possible Theories for Usability Engineering

Usability engineering can be grounded in different theories. Reiterer (2000) introduces a useful classification which differentiates between the craft, cognitive psychology, usability engineering, and technologist approaches. Table 2.1 sets out their different philosophies.

The term "usability engineering" is not defined consistently. Mayhew (1999) defines it as the "discipline that provides structured methods for achieving usability in user interface design during product development." According to Faulkner (2000), "usability engineering is an approach to the development of software and systems which involves user participation from the outset and guarantees the usefulness of the product through the use of a usability specification and metrics."

In the literature, the terms "usability engineering", "user interface design and development", "user-centered design", and "user interaction design" are ambiguous and mutually interchangeable. A useful differentiation was provided by Hix

A. Seffah, E. Metzker, *Adoption-centric Usability Engineering*,
DOI 10.1007/978-1-84800-019-3_2, © Springer-Verlag London Limited 2009

Table 2.1 UI development approaches and underlying philosophies

Theory	Philosophy	Quality achieved via
Craft	Craft: Design through skill and experience	Talent
Cognitive Psychology	Applied science: Apply theory of human information processing	Theory
Usability Engineering	Engineering: Incorporate Human–Computer Interaction (HCI) issues into software engineering	Methods
Technologist	Engineering: Automate or support the engineering process	Tools

and Hartson (Hix and Hartson, 1993). According to their definition, the process of user interface development is decomposed into a behavioral and a constructional component.

In the behavioral component, the interaction is described abstractly in terms of behavior between the user and the system as they interact. This part of the process is called "human–computer interaction development".

In the constructional component, the interaction is described in terms of algorithms, data flow, widgets, and user interface description languages. The constructional part is called "user interface software development". Hix and Hartson point out that there is a conceptual gap between the behavioral and the constructional aspects of user interface development (Hix and Hartson, 1993).

Software development is the core activity of software engineering. Software engineering additionally comprises special activities and techniques for managing, estimating, scheduling and budgeting projects. An analogous relation exists between user interface development and usability engineering.

Figure 2.1 shows the scope of the concepts and how they are related to each other. The development phases depicted in the center row of the figure are the basic steps in all engineering processes. They serve here as landmarks for the scope of the usability engineering and software engineering concepts, with respect to the overall engineering process. However, they are not meant to indicate any temporal dependencies of activities.

2.2 Pure Usability Engineering Methods

Unfortunately, the terms "usability", "methodology", "method" and "technique" are used inconsistently and interchangeably in the scientific literature and in industry practices. In this book we use the definitions in the IEEE Standard Glossary of Software Engineering Terminology (IEEE Std.610.12, 1990). A software development methodology is defined as (IEEE Std.610.12, 1990):

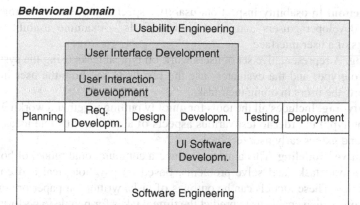

Fig. 2.1 Scope of usability engineering process concepts

1. An integrated set of policies, procedures, rules, standards, techniques, tools, languages, and other methodologies for analyzing, designing, implementing, and testing software; and
2. A set of rules for selecting the correct method and the underlying process and tools

Based on this standard, usability engineering methodologies are software development methodologies with a special emphasis on optimizing the usability of the system that is to be developed. Examples include the Star Lifecycle (Hix and Hartson, 1993) Usability Engineering (Nielsen, 1994), LUCID (Logical User-Centered Interface Design Method) (Smith and Dunckley, 1997), the Usability Engineering Lifecycle (Mayhew, 1999), Usage-Centered Design (Constantine and Lockwood, 1999), MUSE (Method for Usability Engineering) (Lim and Long, 1994), the Nabla Model (Kolski and Loslever, 1998), and SEP (Scenario-based Engineering Process) (McGraw and Harbison, 1997).

Examples of usability engineering techniques include affinity diagramming (Constantine and Lockwood, 1999), usability inspections (Nielsen, 1994), heuristic evaluation (Nielsen, 1994), task analysis (Mayhew, 1999), wizard-of-oz studies, and cognitive walkthroughs (Polson et al., 1992).

2.2.1 A Taxonomy of the Most Popular Usability Engineering (UE) Methods

There is generally seven types of evaluation methods:

1. **Inquiry**. Usability evaluators obtain information about users' likes, dislikes, and understanding of the system by talking to them, observing them using the system in a real working environment, or letting them answer questions verbally or in written form.

2. **Inspection**. In usability inspection, usability specialists – and sometimes software developers, users and other professionals – examine usability-related aspects of a user interface.
3. **Testing**. A representative set of users work on typical tasks using the system (or the prototype) and the evaluators use the results to see how the user interface supports the users in doing their tasks.
4. **Prototyping**. Includes all the tools for quickly putting together a working model (a prototype) in order to test various aspects of a design, illustrate ideas or features and gather early user feedback.
5. **Cognitive Modeling**. This aims to produce a computational model of how people perform tasks and solve problems, based on psychological and cognitive principles. These models can be outlines of tasks written on paper or computer programs which enable us to predict the time it takes for people to perform tasks, the kinds of errors they make, the decisions they make, or what buttons and menu items they choose.
6. **User Requirements Analysis**. The purposes of usability methods at this stage are to collect information about the user interface, users, tasks and environments, and to agree what aspects should be formalized as requirements.
7. **Analytical and Predictive Methods**. These require a designer to predict how a user will react when presented with a User Interface (UI) component or a complete UI, in an attempt to make it as easy and intuitive to use as possible. Because of this method's user focus and the fact that it can be supported by design guidelines, it is generally used to develop initial and early designs or task models.

Table 2.2 gives examples of methods for each of these categories. Each technique has advantages and disadvantages, and there are many ways to classify each method. A method can be used for a different purpose at different stages of the development lifecycle, from requirements to deployment and final usability testing. In the next section, we discuss this issue.

2.2.2 Expert-Based Evaluation

The following methods are the most popular applied techniques for expert-based evaluation and inspection.

Heuristic evaluation. Also known as expert evaluation, this method is used to identify potential problems that operators can be expected to experience when using a computer or a telecommunications application. Analysts evaluate the system with reference to established guidelines or principles, noting down their observations and often ranking them in order of severity. The analysts are usually experts in human factors or Human–Computer Interaction (HCI), but less experienced evaluators have also been shown to report valid problems.

Table 2.2 Taxonomy and examples of UE methods

Category	Popular methods
Inquiry	– Contextual inquiry
	– Ethnographic study/Field study
	– Observation
	– Interzviews
	– Focus groups
	– Survey
	– Questionnaires
	– Self-reporting logs
	– Screen snapshots
Inspection	– Heuristic evaluation
	– Cognitive walkthroughs
	– Formal usability inspections
	– Feature inspection
	– Consistency inspection
	– Standards inspection
	– Guidelines and checklists
Testing	– Thinking aloud protocol
	– Co-discovery method
	– Question-asking protocol
	– Performance measurement
	– Eye tracking
Prototyping	– Paper, Pictive and video prototyping
	– Storyboarding
	– Scenario sketching
Cognitive modeling	– Affinity diagrams
	– Archetypes and personae
	– Blind voting
	– Card sorting
	– Education evaluation
User requirements analysis	– Task analysis
	– Contextual inquiry
	– Focus groups and surveys
	– Personae and scenarios
	– Use case maps
	– Affinity diagramming
	– Brainstorming
	– Card sorting
Analytical and predictive methods	– Goals, Operators, Methods, and Selection (GOMS) performance analysis
	– Cognitive task analysis
	– Task-environment analysis
	– Knowledge analysis
	– Design analysis
	– Programmable user models
	– Simulations

Usability walkthrough. Users, developers and usability specialists individually review a set of designs, and then meet to discuss each element of the design in a walkthrough meeting. Problems and their severity are identified and noted.

2.2.3 Prototyping Techniques

For early prototyping, the following techniques are generally used:

Paper prototyping. Designers create a paper-based simulation of interface elements (menus, dialogues, icons etc.) using paper and pen. When the paper prototype has been prepared, a member of the design team sits before a user and plays the role of the computer by moving interface elements around in response to the user's actions. The difficulties encountered by the user and the user's comments are recorded by an observer and/or audio/video tape recorder.

Video prototyping. This technique is a variant of paper-prototyping that makes use of video equipment to create short movies of the paper interface as the elements are moved by members of the design team. End-users do not interact directly with the paper prototype but can view the video. This approach can be useful for demonstrating interface layout and the dynamics of navigation, particularly to larger audiences.

Computer-based prototyping. This approach to prototyping utilizes computer simulations to provide a more realistic mock-up of the system under development. The representations often have greater fidelity to the finished system than is possible with simple paper mock-ups. Again, end-users interact with the prototype to accomplish set tasks; any problems that arise are noted.

Wizard-of-oz prototyping. This method is a variant of computer-based prototyping and involves the user interacting with a computer system that is actually operated by a hidden developer – referred to as the "wizard". The human wizard processes input from the user and simulates system output. The approach is particularly suited to exploring design possibilities in systems that are demanding to implement, such as intelligent interfaces, which feature agents, advisors and/or natural language processing.

2.2.4 Usability Testing

For usability testing and in particular for user performance evaluation, the following are some of the techniques generally used:

User-based observation to obtain design feedback. This is a relatively quick and cheap way to conduct an empirical evaluation of a working system or prototype, with the emphasis on the acquisition of design feedback information. A small number of participants work individually with system while an observer makes notes. The technique can be used to identify the most significant user-interface problems, but it is not intended to provide reliable metrics.

User-based observation to obtain metrics. This method is specifically aimed at deriving metric data and as such represents a more rigorous form of the preceding method. The real-world working environment and the product under development are simulated as closely as possible. Users undertake realistic tasks while observers make notes, tasks are timed and video and/or audio recordings made. The observations are subsequently analyzed to derive metrics. Design problems are also identified.

Cooperative evaluation. Users employ a prototype as they work through task scenarios in collaboration with other users. They explain what they are doing by talking or "thinking aloud" and this is recorded on tape and/or captured by an observer. The observer also prompts users when they are quiet and actively questions the users with respect to their intentions and expectations.

Supportive evaluation. A participatory form of evaluation; users and developers meet together and the user representatives try to use the system to accomplish set tasks. Users identify issues in a facilitated discussion, and designers can later explore these issues. Several trials can be run to focus on different system features or different versions of the system.

2.2.5 Subjective Assessment

For subjective assessment and for measuring user satisfaction in particular, the following techniques are exploited:

Questionnaires. The Software Usability Measurement Inventory (SUMI) is a prime example of the use of questionnaires to collect subjective feedback. After using the system, participants fill in a standardized 50-statement psychometric questionnaire and their answers are analyzed with the aid of a computer program. As well as providing a global assessment of usability, SUMI data offers information on:

- Perceived efficiency
- Affect (likeability)
- Control
- Learnability
- Helpfulness
- And how these results compare with results for similar software (deduced from a database of past results).

The Questionnaire for User Interface Satisfaction (QUIS) is another subjective assessment questionnaire. This questionnaire focuses directly on the user interface and was developed by Ben Schneiderman and colleagues in the late 1980s. It consists of five sections, where the first assesses the user's overall reactions to the software and the other four assess screen design and layout, terminology and system information, learning, and system capabilities.

Cognitive workload. Measuring cognitive workload involves assessing how much mental effort a user expends in using a prototype or deployed system. For example, this can be obtained from questionnaires such as the Subjective Mental Effort Questionnaire (SMEQ) and the Task Load Index (TLX). The SMEQ uses a single scale, which measures the amount of effort people feel they have invested in a given task. The TLX uses six scales (mental, physical, temporal, performance, effort and frustration) to measure the individual's perception of their task experience. It is also possible to collect objective data from heart rate and respiration rate.

Focus groups. These bring together various stakeholders in the context of a facilitated but informal discussion group. Views are elicited by the facilitator on topics of relevance to the software product being evaluated. Focus groups can be used to identify initial requirements and also serve as a means of collecting feedback once a system has been in use. Several focus groups can be run to concentrate on different topics or to include the views of different sections of the user community.

Individual interviews. These are a quick and inexpensive way to obtain subjective feedback from users based on their practical experience of a product. The interviewer can base their questions on a pre-specified list of items or allow the user to freely provide their views. These are referred to as structured and unstructured interviews respectively. Alternatively a combination of these approaches can be practiced, which results in a semi-structured interview. Interviews are often employed in conjunction with some of the other methods discussed in this handbook, particularly where de-briefing sessions take place.

2.3 UE Methods and the Development Lifecycle

There have been several attempts to classify usability methods according to UCD (User-Centered Design) activities and in general according to the entire software development lifecycle. The following figure summarizes the application of UCD techniques to support the main activities identified in the ISO 13407 standards. The following frameworks portrays at which stages of the development lifecycle, the most popular usability engineering methods can be applied (Fig. 2.2).

Some evaluation techniques, such as formal user testing, can be applied only after the interface design or prototype has been implemented. Others, such as heuristic evaluation, can be applied in the early stages of design. Each technique has its own requirements, and generally different techniques reveal different usability problems.

Here are some tips for choosing and differentiating between the different UE methods.

- Number and characteristics of users
- Number and profile of observers
- Required infrastructure and software
- Testing process including the time and location of test sessions, the type and percentage of problems, and number of iterations

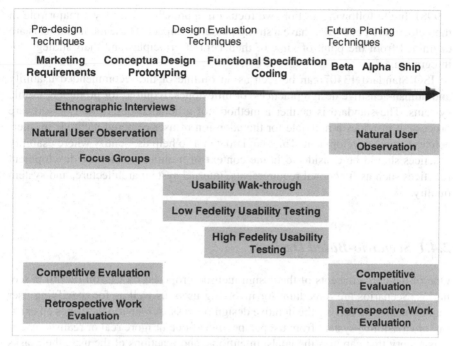

| Pre-design Techniques | | Design Evaluation Techniques | | Future Planing Techniques | | |

Fig. 2.2 Usability methods and the development lifecycle

- Required expertise to analyze the test results and transform user feedback into design recommendations according to the applicable stages of development (based on the planning, early and late categorization of lifecycle stages). The required skill level and number of analysts can vary depending on the method
- Minimum and maximum level of expertise of analysts for the particular method
- Number of users, developers and stakeholders required
- Number of user days required to apply the method

2.4 Other Usability Engineering-Sensitive Methodologies

In addition to the UE methods listed in the above section, a large number of UE-sensitive methodologies have been proposed. These include the Star Lifecycle (Hix and Hartson, 1993), the Logical User-Centered Interface Design Method (LUCID) (Smith and Dunckley, 1997), the Usability Engineering Lifecycle (Mayhew, 1999), Usage-Centered Design (Constantine and Lockwood 1999), SEP (for user-centered requirements using scenarios) (McGraw and Harbison 1997) and IBM-OVID (Object, View, Interaction and Design) (Roberts, 1998).

Reviewing all of these UCD-sensitive methods here would go beyond the scope of this book. Some of these methods, and in particular those aiming to bridge object-oriented models, scenarios and task models are detailed in Artim and VanHarmelen

(1998). In the following section, we focus on approaches that play a major role in the field, or are believed to have a strong potential impact. These methodologies are examined from the point of view of their central principles and their strategy for integration.

ISO Standard 13407 can be seen as an outline of the recommended usability and human-sensitive design practices, or milestones, required for producing usable systems. The standard is neither a method nor a detailed description of software process. It provides a rationale for the adoption of user-centered methods in inter-active systems development. This standard can also help us identify where usability practices should be considered in the context of traditional software development practices such as functional requirements, internal system architecture, and system quality.

2.4.1 Scenario-Based Design

One of the core concepts of the design method proposed by Carroll (2000) is sce-narios. Scenarios are a medium for involving users as well as for specifying user requirements and driving the iterative design process. A scenario describes an exist-ing or envisioned system from the perspective of one or more real or realistic users. It is a story that captures the goals, intentions, and reactions of the user, their tasks and the context in which the system will be used.

Scenarios have several merits. In particular, scenarios can improve and mediate the communication between users, designers and stakeholders. As previously men-tioned, communication with different groups involved in the design process is one of the major integration obstacles. Because scenarios are formulated in simple natural language, they have the advantage of being understood both by users and designers. This enables all project participants to share the design process and discuss potential solutions.

Claims are another core artifact that can complement scenarios. Claims are a form of extended, psychologically motivated design rationale. They express a design principle, with usability and utility tradeoffs, set in a context of use by a scenario, with a specific design that exemplifies the principle (Sutcliffe, 2001). Claims are developed in parallel to scenarios. The core elements that are addressed in a sce-nario are listed with their potential advantages and drawbacks. A claim clarifies which effects each element has on the usability of the system. If the drawbacks of an element outweigh the advantages, it is usually discarded. An example of such a claim for a safety-critical application is given in Table 2.3.

2.4.2 Contextual Design

Contextual design, developed by Beyer and Holtzblatt (1998), stresses the behav-ioral aspects of the system design process. In their view, almost all of the system

Table 2.3 Example of a claim

Claim: Safety-critical application
Claim ID: Rare event monitor.

Target artifact: User interface for a chemical analysis instrument control system.

Description: Infrequent, dangerous events are detected by the system and a warning is issued to the user; in this case operational failures in a laser gas chromatograph control system.

Upside: Automatic detection of dangerous events relieves the user of constant monitoring; automatic detection and warning gives the user time to analyze the problem.

Downside: Issuing too many warnings may lead the user to ignore critical events; automated monitoring may lead to user overconfidence in the automated system and decrease their situation awareness.

Scenario: No events are detected in the laser emission controller or power supply, so the system gives an audio warning to the user and visually signals the location of the problem on a diagram of the instrument.

design process is driven by behavioral issues. Software requirements engineering, as a subsequent phase, is viewed as a response to the system design process. In other words, the complete system design process should be an input to the software requirements engineering process. The key activities of contextual design are: observe and interview the customer, construct and consolidate work models, redesign work models, and design the system.

Beyer and Holtzblatt (1998) emphasize that "the ability to see, manipulate, and design a process for delivering systems is a fundamental skill when it comes to establishing their techniques in software development processes". However, they provide only very generic recommendations for adapting the overall approach to different project configurations. They recommend, for example, recognizing "which parts are critical and which are less necessary in each case", understanding that "what works for a two-person team won't work for a fifteen person team", "what works to design a strategy for a new market venture won't work for the next iteration of a 10-year old system", and that in adapting the approach it is important to "tailor things you pick up to your problem, team and organization" and there is the comment that "what you do with it is up to you" (Beyer and Holtzblatt, 1998).

2.4.3 Star Lifecycle

The Star lifecycle proposed by Hix and Hartson (1993) focuses on usability evaluation as the hub process activity. Placed around this central task are the following activities: (1) system, task, functionality, user analysis, requirements and usability specifications, (2) design, design representation, and rapid prototyping, (3) software production and deployment. The results of each activity are submitted to an evaluation before moving on to the next process activity. It is possible to start with almost any development activity. The bi-directional links between the central usability evaluation task and all other process activities cause the graphical representation of the model to assume a star shape.

One of the drawbacks of this approach has been outlined by Hix and Hartson (Hix and Hartson, 1993). Project managers tend to have problems with the highly iterative nature of the model: they find it difficult to decide when a specific iteration is completed. This decision difficulty complicates the management of resources and limits the ability to control the overall progress of the development process. An obvious solution to this problem is to establish control mechanisms such as quantitative usability goals that serve as stopping rules.

Hix and Hartson provide some basic advice on tailoring the overall approach to a specific development context. If the development team has experience with and prior knowledge of the target system structure, they suggest a top-down approach. Otherwise they favor a more experimental bottom-up approach. They suggest that the overall approach should be configured to accommodate the size of the project, the number of people involved, and the management style.

Hix and Hartson explicitly emphasize the necessity to view usability engineering as a process, but they agree that the design phase is one of the least understood development activities. They provide special methods and notations to support the process. For example, the user action notation (UAN) specifies user interaction in a way that is easily readable and yet unambiguous for implementing the actual interface. Usability specification tables are employed for defining and tracing quantitative usability goals.

2.4.4 Usability Engineering Lifecycle

Proposed by Deborah Mayhew, the usability engineering lifecycle is an attempt to redesign the complete software development process around usability engineering knowledge, methods, and activities (Mayhew, 1999). This process starts with a structured requirements analysis concerning usability issues. The data gathered from the requirements analysis are used to define explicit, measurable usability goals for the proposed system.

The usability engineering lifecycle accomplishes the defined usability goals via an iteration of usability engineering methods such as conceptual model design, user interface mock-ups, prototyping and usability testing. The iterative process terminates if the usability goals have been met or if the resources allocated for the task have been consumed.

As outlined by Mayhew (1999), the usability engineering lifecycle has been applied successfully in a number of projects. However, some general drawbacks were discovered by Mayhew during these case studies. One key concern is that redesigning the overall development process around usability issues often poses a problem to the organizational culture of software engineering organizations. The well-established development processes of an organization cannot easily be turned into human-centered processes during a single project. Furthermore, development teams often have insufficient knowledge to perform the UE activities, which hampers the establishment of UE activities in the engineering processes.

Precisely how the UE activities proposed in the usability engineering lifecycle should be integrated smoothly into engineering processes practiced by software development organizations was declared by Mayhew to be an open research issue. Mayhew names several success factors for practicing UE. In particular, all project team members should carry out UE process steps. Mayhew stresses the importance of ultimately formalizing UE within a development organization and methodology. Project team participation is necessary and having a design guru on board is not enough.

2.4.5 Usage-Centered Design

Usage-centered design, developed by Constantine and Lockwood (1999) , is based on a process model called the activity model for usage-centered design. The activity model starts in parallel with the activities of collaborative requirements modeling, task modeling, and domain modeling in order to elicit basic requirements of the planned software system. The requirements analysis phase is followed by the design activities of interface content modeling and implementation modeling.

These activities are continuously repeated until the system passes the usability inspections carried out after each iteration. The design and test activities are paralleled by the help system and documentation development and standards definition for the proposed system. This general framework of activities is supplemented by special methods such as essential use case models and user role maps.

Constantine and Lockwood cite many case studies where usage centered design was successfully applied, yet they encountered many of the same organizational obstacles as Mayhew (1999) when integrating their UE approach into the software engineering processes in practice. They concluded that new practices, processes, and tools have to be introduced into the organization and then spread beyond the point of introduction.

A straightforward solution to these problems is the establishment of training courses for all participants of UE activities offered by external consultants. However, this solution is regarded as time-consuming and cost intensive in the long run. Also, it tends to have only a temporary effect and thus does not promote organizational learning in UE design methods. Constantine and Lockwood conclude that it is necessary to build up an internal body of knowledge concerning UE methods, best practices and tools, in a way that is tailored to the needs of the development organization.

2.5 Extensions to Traditional Software Engineering Methods

Whereas the previous sections focused on methods proposed by the HCI community, another approach to integrating UE with software engineer (SE) practices is to extend existing SE processes and artifacts. This is particularly useful in the context where we are trying to solve the integration problem for organizations that already have a software development process or practice in place.

This section will review proposals to identify and resolve the overlaps and similarities between UE and SE artifacts and techniques, as well as attempts to integrate usability into well-established SE methods such as the Rational Unified Process or the more recent agile methods.

In particular, this section looks at the relationships among scenarios (Carroll, 2000; Benyon and Macaulay 2002), use cases (Cockburn, 1997); (Seffah and Hayne 1999); (Constantine, 1999), object-oriented notations such as Unified Modeling Language (UML) (Paterno, 2001); (Krutchen, 1999); (Pinheiro et al., 2001); (Markopoulos and Marijnissen, 2000) and task models (Artim and VanHarmelen 1998); (Dayton et al., 1998); (Rosson, 1999); (Paterno, 2001); (Forbrig, 1999). These investigations propose solutions to some of the major integration issues, in particular for integrating UE practices into object-oriented methodologies.

Proposed solutions include:

* Extending software engineering artifacts for UI specification, such as annotating use cases with task descriptions (Constantine, 1999); (Rosson, 1999); (Cockburn, 1997); (Dayton et al., 1998)
* Enhancing object-oriented software engineering notations and models (Nunes and Cunha 2000); (Artim and VanHarmelen, 1998); (Krutchen, 1999); (Pinheiro et al., 2001)
* Possible extensions of Human-Centered Design (HCD) methods for requirements gathering through field observations and interviews; deriving a conceptual design model from scenario, task models and use cases (Rosson et al., 2001); (Paterno, 2001); (Benyon and Macaulay 2002); and using personae (Cooper et al., 2007) as a way to understand and model end-users
* New methodologies for interactive systems design such as (Mayhew, 1999); (Roberts, 1998), as well as approaches complementing existing methodologies (Constantine and Lockwood, 1999); (Krutchen, 1999)

These investigations demonstrate that in use-case driven software development, HCD processes in general and task analysis approaches in particular are highly compatible. This is a starting point for cross-pollinating functional and user requirements engineering techniques and tools. For example, user-centered requirement artifacts such as task and user models can substantially improve certain basic weaknesses of the functional requirements approach, such as identifying the context of use.

2.5.1 Adding Usage Scenarios to Object-Oriented Analysis and Design

As an artifact for capturing user requirements, scenarios have been promoted both in HCI (Carroll, 2000) and software engineering (Jarke, 1999). However, the concept of scenarios has not been consistently defined. Jarke (1999) proposes to clarify the purpose and method of using scenarios in the modeling process, since scenarios can be used in very different ways. Jarke points out that scenarios are used in software engineering as intermediate design artifacts (Jarke, 1999) while Carroll argues that scenarios can be used as a driving force in the entire design process.

Rosson (1999) suggests enhancing the object-oriented analysis and design approach with a scenario-based approach. Once scenarios are completed, she proposes first extracting elements that are potential computational objects, and then organizing them as a network of collaborating objects. The next step is to focus on a specific object and try to assign functionality to it. This object-by-object analysis is supported by the Point-Of-View Browser that maintains user-relative descriptions of each object.

This design approach is middle-out, since it iteratively elaborates a set of user tasks (described in user interaction scenarios) in two directions: toward networks of collaborating computational objects on the one hand, and toward detailed user interaction episodes on the other. This is the opposite of prototyping tools such as Visual Basic, which are outside in, because the focus is on screen design.

Rosson's approach ensures a good object model as well as satisfying the need to take into account the user's point of view. It also addresses our main concern: the incorporation of the user's needs into the software development process. However, in this technique the user interface design relies only on the user's description of their tasks and usability claims. Rosson acknowledges that this can cause mismatches with the user's view, but she explains that these mismatches are minor compared to the need for structure in the task model.

Thus Rosson defines an intermediate philosophy. The aim is not exclusively the user and their needs, or a good structure of the software; the aim is to have a good midpoint construct that helps establish a good user interface as well as a good program structure. This solution has not become popular in the industry market, perhaps because it is too different from the methods currently in use.

Similar to Rosson's work, Jarke (1999) also proposes clarifying the purpose and method for using scenarios in the modeling process. He defines scenarios as constructs that describe a possible set of events that might reasonably take place; these scenarios offer "middle-ground abstraction between models and reality". Scenarios can communicate:

- A sequence of work activities
- A sequence of end-user representations or interfaces
- The purpose of users in the use of the software
- The lifecycle of the product

One of the major weaknesses of scenarios as an integration artifact is the fact that informal representations of scenarios, generally statements in natural language, are often insufficient for overcoming the difficulty of communication between users, developers, usability experts and stakeholders with differing backgrounds. Scenarios in natural languages suffer from ambiguity and imprecision.

Formal representations of scenarios provide a solution to the ambiguity problem and facilitate formal proof and analysis of properties of requirements. However, for newcomers to structured representations, these formal specifications are often difficult to understand and develop.

A trade-off is needed between the precision of formal representations and the ease of communication of scenarios in the context of accomplishing a task. Designers and users need to be able to develop and reason about scenario descriptions throughout the development lifecycle in a variety of media, purposes, and views, either to discuss existing options or to stimulate imagination.

2.5.2 Task Analysis Versus Object-Oriented and Use Cases Models

In model-based task analysis as practiced in HCI, the objective is normally to achieve a generic and thus abstract model of user tasks, typically in a hierarchical form of goals, subgoals and methods for achieving the hierarchy of goals. In object-oriented development, use cases are often employed in gathering functional requirements.

Can task analysis models be improved by use case techniques? Can use cases be improved by the incorporation or consideration of formal task models? Are there ways of integrating the two approaches? Such questions have been widely discussed (Dayton et al., 1998); (Artim and VanHarmelen, 1998); (Seffah and Hayne, 1999); (Forbrig, 1999).

Cockburn (1997), for one, recognizes that use-cases are not well defined and many different uses coexist, with differences in purpose, content, plurality and structure. He proposes to structure them with respect to goals or tasks. Although this approach may appear unusual as a structure for requirements, it follows a natural hierarchical organization typical of task analysis techniques (Dayton et al., 1998). The goals are structured as a tree containing "Summary goals" as high-level goals, and "User goals" as atomic goals (e.g. performing summary goal A involves performing user goal A1 then A2).

Because of the similarities between use cases and task analysis (Artim and Van-Harmelen, 1998); (Seffah and Hayne 1999); (Rosson, 1999), software and usability engineers often try to substitute one for the other, without realizing that the two tools are designed differently in order to accomplish different purposes.

2.5.3 UML Notation for User Interface Modeling

Several research investigations have been conducted with a view to improving the UML for user interfaces and interactive systems engineering. Nunes and Cunha (2000) propose the Whitewater Interactive System Development with Objects Models (WISDOM), as a lightweight software engineering methodology that uses UML to support Human–Computer interaction techniques. WISDOM is evolutionary in the sense that the project evolves incrementally through an iterative process. A novel aspect of this work is the addition of extensions to UML to accommodate task analysis. The modeling constructs include:

- A description of users and their relevant characteristics
- A description of user behavior/intentions in performing the envisioned or supported task
- A specification of the abstract and concrete user interface

WISDOM applies many changes and additions to UML to support this: change of class stereotype boundary, control and entity; addition of task, interaction space, class stereotype; add-ons of the associations "communicate", "subscribe", "refine task", "navigate", "contains", etc. The communication scheme here appears to be a "co-evolutionary development of interactive systems", i.e. having models evolve in parallel. But concerns arise about the frequent communication misadventures between HCI and Software Engineering specialists, as well as the tendency to misinterpret constructs such as use-cases, caused by different cultures having a different understanding of a versatile language like UML.

In the same vein as this work, Markopoulos (Markopoulos and Marijnissen, 2000) and Pinheiro (Pinheiro et al., 2001) also propose extensions to UML for interactive systems. In contrast, a task is represented as classes in WISDOM and by activities in the Unified Modeling Language Interface (UMLi) framework proposed by (Pinheiro et al., 2001). Paterno (2002) also suggests an extension of their task-modeling notation, Concurrent Task Tree (CTT).

The above research shows that UML suffers from a lack of support for User Interface (UI) modeling. For example, class diagrams are not entirely suitable for modeling interaction, which is a major component in HCI. The IBM-OVID (Object, View, Interaction and Design) methodology is an attempt to provide an iterative process for developing an object-oriented model by refining and transforming a task model (Roberts, 1998).

2.5.4 Enhancing Use Cases for User Interface Prototyping

Artim (Artim and VanHarmelen, 1998), Constantine and Lockwood (Constantine and Lockwood, 1999) and (Krutchen, 1999) all augment use cases to support interface design and prototyping. This integration is based on the synchronization of the problem specification and the solution specification; these two specifications are updated at each iteration through an assessment of impact of the changes in the models.

Theoretically, having a consistent use case model that provides simple views for any actor and automatically includes the user's concerns should be enough to enable software engineers to keep track of the users' needs during the design process. However, as Artim and the participants in his workshop pointed out (Artim and VanHarmelen, 1998), the culture of software engineering does not include collaborating with the user in the process of building a better system.

These sociological forces within development teams severely limit the user's impact in the development of the system, resulting in a system that fits to user interface specifications, rather than optimizing the fit to the user's needs. Thus, even though the development method directly determines the product being created, it is not the only factor.

Constantine and Lockwood (1999) aim to harness the potential of use-cases by having them supplement task models and scenarios. They first recapitulate requirements by structuring the models into five interrelated components:

- User Role Map, structuring the user roles (which hold the user information)
- Navigation Map, structuring the content models (which hold the interface views)
- Use Case Map, structuring the use cases (which hold the task descriptions)
- Domain Model, which holds glossary, data and class models
- Operational Model, which holds environmental and contextual factors

These sets of models and maps can be developed or enhanced in parallel, which departs from more traditional (albeit iterative) sequential approaches.

In the attempt to completely specify the design methodology, Constantine and Lockwood define the notion of essential use-cases. These essential use-cases enhance usability by focusing on intention rather than interaction, and simplification rather than elaboration. The essential use-cases provide an inventory of user intentions and system responsibilities, focusing only on information considered essential and hiding unneeded information; this approach helps use-cases adapt to eventual technological or environmental changes.

Constantine and Lockwood give a structure to essential use-cases, at the same time defining the syntax of the narratives. They also acknowledge the limitations of essential use-cases in the domain of software engineering; for this reason they advocate the use of essential use-cases only in the core process, where usability characteristics are essential.

Krutchen (1999) proposes to add a new artifact to the Rational Unified Process: the use-case storyboard. This artifact provides a high-level view of dynamic relationships in the user interface such as window navigation paths and other navigation paths between objects in the user interface. Use-case storyboards are written at analysis time, at the same time as the use-cases. They include a number of useful constructs such as:

- Flows of events, also called storyboards. These are textual user-centered descriptions of interactions.
- Class Diagrams. These are classes that participate in the use-cases.
- Interaction Diagrams. These describe the collaboration between objects.
- Usability Requirements. These are textual version of usability requirements.
- References to the User-Interface Prototype. This is a text description of the user-interface prototype.
- Trace dependency. This is a map of the use cases.

Krutchen (1999) also proposes guidelines on how to use this new construct. He recommends that a human-factors expert should write these storyboards, because traditional software engineers, not being used to the philosophy of these storyboards, will not design or use this artifact correctly.

A concern about this new technique comes from its practice of specifying the interface at the beginning, rather than deriving them from a design model, thus "putting the cart before the horse" and limiting the possibilities of the interface (Constantine and Lockwood, 1999). This also illustrates that use-cases can adapt to usability engineering, but there is no assurance that designers will use them appropriately.

Chapter 3
Pitfalls and Obstacles in the Integration and Adoption Path

Taking into account usability in the software development lifecycle is not an easy endeavor. The issue of integrating usability engineer (UE) and software engineer (SE) processes and practices was the main topic of several workshops organized during the last decade as well as a number of research efforts. The starting point of all these workshops was the two workshops organized by Artim et al. at CHI'97 and CHI'98 conferences on Object-Oriented Models in User Interface Design and on incorporating Task Analysis Into Commercial And Industrial Object-Oriented Systems Development (Artim, 1997); (Artim and VanHarmelen, 1998). These workshops highlighted the UE and SE gaps and the importance of addressing them (Artim, 1997); (Artim and VanHarmelen, 1998); (Seffah and Hayne, 1999); (Nunes, 2000); (Gulliksen et al., 1999); (Kazman et al., 2003). These workshops demonstrated also that the integration of usability into software engineering should be considered at different levels including the product, process, and organizational/cultural perspectives. However, the integration path is littered with major fallacies, myths and obstacles that have hampered efforts to bridge Human–Computer Interaction (HCI) and SE concerns together in an integrative perspective. Here, we summarize some of the major obstacles; an exhaustive discussion of the obstacles can be found in Seffah and Metzker (2004).

3.1 The Fallacious Dichotomy Between User Interface and System Functionality

As described at the beginning of this chapter, software engineers have aimed at separating user interface (UI) concerns from the underlying software systems that support the functionality while also aiming to increase reusability, scalability, and usability. To a large extent, they have succeeded. We now build applications that can dynamically adapt their "look and feel" to different windowing systems at almost no cost.

The term "user interface" is perhaps one of the underlying obstacles in the quest for usable programs since it gives the impression of a thin layer sitting on top of the other software that is the "real" system. This dichotomy explains the "peanut

A. Seffah, E. Metzker, *Adoption-centric Usability Engineering*,
DOI 10.1007/978-1-84800-019-3_3, © Springer-Verlag London Limited 2009

butter theory of usability" (Lewis and Rieman, 2001). Lewis explains that usability is often seen as:

> ... *A spread that can be smeared over any software model, however dreadful, with good results if the spread is thick enough. If the underlying functionality is confusing, then spread a graphical user interface on it. ... If the user interface still has some problems, smear some manuals over it. If the manuals are still deficient, smear on some training which you force users to take.*

Other common misconceptions, beliefs and attitudes that hamper a successful establishment of usability engineering techniques are that "user interface design tasks do not arise until the detailed design phase of a development project" and that "user interface design can be done right the first time, in the design phase" (Mayhew, 1999).

Many software engineers believe that well-established techniques of developing software in general can be applied equally well to user interface development. However, as Hix and Hartson pointed out, user interface development consists of human–computer interaction development and user interface software development (Hix and Hartson, 1993). The second of these can be done entirely using UI toolkits or Graphical User Interface(GUI)-Builders, but the first – human–computer interaction development – cannot.

These efforts to separate the UI from the underlying application have led to the misconception that both can evolve independently, or that we can design a system without immediate concern for its UI. The role of the user interface is often perceived as that of decorating a thin component sitting on top of the software, with the software being the "real" system. Software engineers build the software and all its functionality, and once the bulk of the work is done, the usability people make the interface layer user-friendly.

The usability people, on the other hand, view their role as designing the interface at the beginning of the project; it is only later on, once all the functionality is defined and validated, that the software engineers implement the back-end to support this design, under constant revision by usability inspectors.

These views of each other's role are of course in direct opposition and often result in frustrations within one group for not being given sufficient influence on the final product. Moreover, to the extent that usability determines which functions are most relevant, how they interrelate within a task and what information should be available to the user for performing a given task, it is ill-conceived to imagine that the UI and the underlying system can evolve independently. They are closely linked. This argument has recently been made that usability scenarios affect the design of the software architecture, for example Bass et al. (2001).

We do believe that usability should be considered both for the whole system and for the design of any specific elements that may influence usability. These elements include:

- The user interface and all of its components
- The system functionalities – especially those that may impact on usability – such as time-consuming features which require to provide continuous feedback

- Help systems and context-sensitive support
- Training resources
- User manuals
- Technical support procedures
- Installation and customization handbook
- Material for trainers, installers, indirect users and stakeholders

In addition to these factors and ensuring usability over a long period of time and between versions, the development portfolio should include the rationale of the major UI decisions, the specific design guidelines and evaluation criteria, as well as the future tests goals. Such information is extremely important when reengineering an interactive system.

3.2 The Cultural Gap Between Psychologists and Engineers

Usability professionals and UI designers, most often possessing a psychology background, are sometimes regarded as mere nuisances who get in the way of the engineers and computer scientists who, in the end, will really deliver the product. User interface development is seldom allocated sufficient time in the crucial early phases of the development schedule, even if the user interface code is often more than half of the whole code for a project and takes a comparable amount of development effort (Myers, 1995).

This "people gap" is exacerbated by the fact that the two groups do not share the same culture including terminology: this can be summarized as the dichotomy of users and HCI versus developers and engineering. These two groups do not share the same perspective and they don't understand the respective constraints under which each group has to operate. It has been our experience that when the UE specialist is also a strong programmer and analyst, UE methods are systematically much better accepted by the software engineers and integrated in the development process.

Figure 3.1 is a visual representation that shows the differences between developers and usability professionals.

Software engineers need to understand and master usability engineering in their own language and cultural context. Usability specialists often don't understand why and how technical choices and constraints influence a product's design.

Seffah (2004) describes a list of 14 HCI design skills that are needed by developers in order for them to do a good job of designing interfaces. The paper recommends establishing several "usability advocates" within the company. The paper also proposes offering a 3-day user interface design workshop in which the project team works with end-users to design part of their project. The UI design workshop is an opportunity for both groups to learn HCI design methods.

Another way for the usability professional to educate technology-driven professionals in user-centered approaches is to provide them with a comprehensive step-by-step framework that lays out the entire process. This is an effective way for software organizations and engineers to learn from usability engineering and at

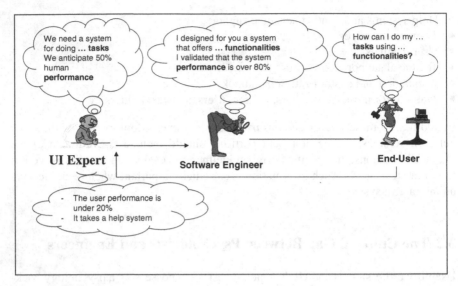

Fig. 3.1 Cultural gap between software engineers and usability expert

the same time to improve collaboration between usability engineering and software engineering.

Some software managers feel that their project can't afford to spend so much time on usability. They worry that the UE-related iterations will never end, due to HCI people trying to get everything perfect. There are two answers to this. Firstly, measurable usability objectives should be set as part of the project plan. And secondly, these managers should consider the longer-term beneficial effects of high-quality work on the job satisfaction, and hence overall productivity, of the organization.

3.3 User-Centeredness is an Organizational Learning Process

The existence of a credible body of evidence concerning the measured value of specific UE methods is often believed to be a prerequisite for organizational learning and process improvement in UE. Unfortunately several surveys on information system methodology research indicate that there are few empirical studies of the effects and acceptance of UE techniques (Glass, 1995); (Zelkowitz, 1996); (Basili et al., 1999).

There is a reason for this lack of empirical evidence. To empirically evaluate the value of a specific UE method, it would be necessary to compare the same project under conditions employing UE techniques versus not employing UE techniques, while controlling for skill, motivation, SE approach and other possible differences between the two project teams. This challenging experiment would need to be repeated many times with different project teams, different software engineering frameworks and on different projects in order for the results to achieve statistical validity.

Therefore to statistically prove the added value of a specific UE method, or of any other traditional software engineering method, in a realistic project context, would cost an overwhelming amount of effort and money. This expense would need to be repeated tens of times to evaluate the full range of UE techniques. Unfortunately there is no funding body wealthy enough to support this research.

In organizational terms, UE must be understood not merely as a process improvement to SE, but as a paradigm shift. In conditions of paradigm shift, those who follow the old paradigm tend to reject new paradigms, even when the new paradigm is heavily supported by scientific evidence (Kuhn, 1962).

Kühn was relatively cynical about paradigm shift, concluding that followers of the old paradigm never convert, and that a successful paradigm shift requires replacing them with followers of the new paradigm. Contemporary management approaches often take the more humanistic position that organizations and individuals can change. The truth likely lies somewhere between these two extremes: Organizations and individuals can change, but change is hard and requires openness and intent.

Ultimately at the corporate level, the decision to employ usability must be based on a clear corporate vision committed to quality, service, and humanity. Without these values, the availability of scientific proof would likely not significantly improve acceptance of usability in an organization. Kühn's observations on paradigm shift strongly support this statement about scientific evidence.

At the project team level, what is most important for acceptance of UE is the availability of techniques that bridge the gap between UE and SE. This combination of top-down (value-bridging) and bottom-up (methodology-bridging) factors ensures the fullest possible success of integrating usability into an organization. Methodology-bridging approaches are discussed in detail in the following chapters.

Although scientific evidence may be less than critical for organizational acceptance of UE, it is very important in helping to decide which UE methods work best. So the current lack of empirical evaluation leads to problems for both researchers and practitioners. As a result, for researchers, valid questions on how to optimally integrate UE techniques into the software development lifecycle are in danger of degenerating into "religious wars" (Paterno, 2001). A prominent recent example is the dispute between the scenario-based and task-based camps (Benyon, 2002).

Such disputes are largely caused by a lack of empirical evidence to support a decision for the deployment of a specific UE technique for a certain class of development projects. Based on which data should a researcher improve or extend a UE technique if empirical data on its acceptance value in practice is not available?

3.4 The Usability of Usability Engineering Methods

Recent studies indicate that UE methods are still not widely adopted by software development teams. A study was conducted in Germany with software engineers who were working on the design of interactive systems in a variety of domains

(DaimlerChrysler Aerospace [DASA] in Ulm, Sony in Fellbach, Grundig in Fuerth and DaimlerChrysler Passenger Car Production in Sindelfingen) (Oed et al., 2001). The study revealed that the examined organizations practiced highly diverse engineering processes.

Furthermore, the study indicated that the people entrusted with the ergonomic analysis and evaluation of interactive systems were primarily the developers of the products. External usability experts and independent in-house usability departments were seldom available. Few of the participants were familiar with methods such as user profile analysis or cognitive walkthroughs, which are regarded as fundamental from a usability engineer's point of view.

A number of case studies examine success factors and potential obstacles for the deployment of UE methodologies in software development processes. They indicate that there is a gap between UE research and the utilization of the research results. Gould and Lewis (1985) found that user-centered design principles were perceived as neither obvious nor intuitive by practitioners. UE methods were not applied nearly as often as they should be. This was primarily due to a lack of knowledge of how to apply User-Centered Design (UCD) principles.

The UE methods which are considered to be reasonable for application by engineers are often not used by them for the following interrelated reasons:

- There is no time allocated for UE activities: these activities are not integrated in the development process or in the project schedule.
- Knowledge needed for the performance of UE tasks is not available within the development team.
- The effort for the application of the UE tasks is estimated to be too high because the tasks are regarded as time-consuming.

These results indicate that it is important to examine how UE methods can be successfully introduced and established. Rosenbaum identifies success factors for establishing UE methods in software development processes (Rosenbaum et al., 2002).

Rosenbaum emphasizes that the core principles of user-centered design should be communicated to the whole project team. Rosenbaum suggests using workshops and tutorials for this purpose. The goal is to gain support not only from mid-level management but also from individual developers. Furthermore, there is a need for a set of highly efficient UE methods that is perceived by the project team as being useful. These UE methods should be integrated into the organization's software development process. The whole project team should be involved in UE practices. Rosenbaum points out that textbook methods such as traditional usability testing often have to be adapted to the context in order to be useful.

The findings of Rosenbaum were confirmed by a study of Vredenburg which examined UE practice across the industry (Vredenburg and Butler, 1996). According to Vredenburg, many UE methods are not effective or practical in practice.

Mao et al. investigated the applied use of UE methods across information technology industries (Mao and Vredenburg, 2001). Their results reinforce the hypothesis that there is a big gap between available research and the use of that research by software engineering practitioners. Usability methods and techniques are not commonly used in practice. This is also true for basic methods such as iterative design and testing on prototypes.

Mao et al. identified several reasons for this situation. First, the resources dedicated to UE issues are very limited. Second, employees resisted UE methods on the individual developer level. Finally, knowledge about user-centered design principles and UE methods was missing in the development teams.

More recent approaches are aimed at making user-centered design more usable. One of the claims of this research stream is that there is a need to make theoretically sound methods available and accessible (Thimbleby, 2000). Furthermore, Gulliksen argues that "practitioners need above all a framework or structure and principles of how to perform UE activities in practice" (Gulliksen et al., 1999).

3.5 The Lack of Process Support Tools

UE is perceived by software development practitioners as tedious and time-consuming (Oed et al., 2001). Process support tools should enable project teams to deploy UE techniques easily and efficiently.

However, development organizations should not be forced to adopt a fixed set of UE techniques; the underlying software engineering processes vary greatly. Instead, any tool introduced should facilitate a smooth integration of UE methods into the individual software development process practiced by the organization.

Turning technology-centered processes into human-centered processes should be seen as a continuous process improvement task where organizations learn which of the available UE methods best match certain engineering contexts. This approach should enable organizations to gradually adopt new UE methods.

It has been observed that the staff entrusted with interface design and evaluation often lack a special background in UE methods. Yet when the need for usability is recognized by the participating organizations, they tend to develop their own in-house usability guidelines and heuristics.

Recent research (Billingsley, 1995); (Rosenbaum et al., 2000); (Spencer, 2000); (Weinschenk and Yeo, 1995) supports the observation that such usability best practices and heuristics are, in fact, compiled and employed by software development organizations. Spencer (2000), for example, presents a streamlined cognitive walkthrough method which has been developed to facilitate efficient performance of cognitive walkthroughs under the social constraints of a large software development organization.

Unfortunately, from experiences collected in the field of software engineering (Basili et al., 1994), it can be assumed that best practices like Spencer's are rarely published either by development organizations or by the scientific community. They are limited to the people of a certain project, or even worse, to one expert member of this group, and this makes the available body of knowledge hard to access. Similar projects in other departments of the organization usually cannot profit from these experiences. In the worst case, the knowledge may leave the organization when the expert changes jobs. Therefore, any tool introduced should not only support existing human-factors methods but also allow the organizations to compile, develop and evolve their own approaches (Metzker and Offergeld, 2001a).

UCD methods should still be regarded as knowledge-intensive. Thus, we need tools to provide engineers with the knowledge of how to effectively perform UE activities. Furthermore, tools should enable software development organizations to explore which of the existing UE methods work best for them in a given project context and how they can refine and evolve basic methods to make them fit into their particular project context. A dynamic model that allows organizations to keep track of the application context of UE methods is called for (Metzker, 2001b).

3.6 Collecting Best Practices in UE is Missing

Recent research shows that even highly interactive systems are frequently developed without the help of in-house human-factors specialists or external usability consultants (Metzker and Offergeld, 2001). For this reason, UE methods often cannot be utilized because the necessary knowledge is not available within the development teams (Mayhew, 1999).

In addition, development organizations with a low usability maturity are often overwhelmed by the sheer complexity of the proposed UE process models. The models lack a defined procedure for tailoring themselves to basic project constraints such as domain, team size, experience level of the development team and type of system engineering process.

Many UE methods exist. The vital importance of tailoring these sets of techniques to project constraints is emphasized in prominent UE methodologies (Bias, 1994); (Nielsen, 1994). Yet we lack empirical data to guide meaningful adaptation to even the most important project factors. Systematic tailoring of methodologies has not yet been addressed in UCD. As it remains unclear how to integrate UE activities in software development processes, they have often been regarded as dispensable and have been skipped when schedules are tight (Mayhew, 1999).

3.7 Educational Gap Between Software Professionals and Usability Professionals

UE specialists, who are usually psychologists, are often regarded as mere nuisances who get in the way of "real" software engineers. The "priest-with-a-parachute" (Hix and Hartson, 1993) image illustrates the role of usability experts in the process: usability people jump into the middle of a project and stay just long enough to give it their blessing. Another metaphor often used is that of "usability police".

The difficulties of communication between the software engineering team and usability specialists can seriously compromise the integration of usability in the software development lifecycle. Among the difficulties in communication, the most notable are the educational gap, the use of different notations, languages, and tools, and the contrasting perception of the role and importance of the design artifacts. For example, in spite of the similarities between use cases and task analysis (Artim and Van Harmelen, 1998); (Forbrig, 1999); (Hayne et al., 1999) and the advantages of their complementary use, software and usability engineers often try to substitute one for the other.

Software engineers need cost-effective educational tools to understand and master usability engineering in their own language and cultural context. One way for the usability professional to educate technology-driven professionals in user-centered approaches would be to provide them with a complete, comprehensive, step-by-step framework that lays out the entire process.

One of the important challenges facing usability specialists is that they are frequently unable to understand the technical choices and constraints that developers are faced with and their effect on a product's design. This situation stems mainly from the lack of a means to mediate communication between usability specialists and software engineers. This mediation is a key point for cross-pollinating the two disciplines and for integrating usability into software development organizations.

Part II
ACUE Fundamentals, Architecture and Components

Chapter 4
Usability Engineering Integration as an Adoption Problem

There is evidence that the large body of knowledge detailed in the previous section often fails to be used, adopted and deployed in industry settings. As discussed in Chapter , important barriers to effective integration and adoption include their unfamiliarity with developers, their lack of maturity, and their limited support for integration. These barriers motivated new research avenues on how usability can be made more easily adopted by inserting them as extensions to commonly used software engineering methods and tools. This chapter discusses these avenues as well as the different possible approaches for the development of an adoption-centric methodology. The question that arises is how can these measurements be gathered without introducing excessive overhead to the development projects? Furthermore, how can the gathered data from different projects be integrated to yield stronger conclusions? How can the data and abstract models of the framework be presented in a form that is useful to software engineering teams? In this chapter these questions are further analyzed. Disciplines that could contribute to a solution are identified. The potential contributions of these disciplines are described.

4.1 Key Milestones in the Adoption Process

Two approaches for deploying, adopting and institutionalizing new methods are possible. The first one, expert-based institutionalization, requires resorting to third-party companies or involving external consultant experts who can help the team acquire, implement and institutionalize the new software engineering methods. The second one, evidence-driven adoption, involves adopting a measurement program for learning about the effectiveness of software engineering methods. The potential benefits of this type of approach are just beginning to be explored. Here, we will focus primarily on the second of these two adoption approaches.

Mayhew (1999) proposes three milestones for adopting software usability engineering methods at an organizational level. These steps are promotion, implementation and institutionalization. Tables 4.1–4.3 summarize these steps while highlighting the organizational and human barriers. None of these obstacles is easy to address. However, failing to recognize and address them will doom the organiza-

A. Seffah, E. Metzker, *Adoption-centric Usability Engineering*,
DOI 10.1007/978-1-84800-019-3_4, © Springer-Verlag London Limited 2009

Table 4.1 Major obstacles in promoting usability engineer (UE) methods

Step	Mains activities	Tips and obstacles
Promotion	Identify and address organizational obstacles to change	Obstacles: – Prevalent myths, beliefs, and attitudes – Organizational incentives and practices – A high visibility of possible disaster – A commitment to address general business goals
	Identify and exploit potential motivators	Tips: – Know your audiences – Cast yourself as an ally, not an enemy – Check the credibility of motivators and their communication skills

Table 4.2 Obstacles in implementing a usability method

Step	Activities	Tips and obstacles
Implementation	– Staffing the function – Organizing the function – Defining roles – Providing career paths – Planning and budgeting	– Focus efforts on the projects of one particular section of the overall development organization – the one that seems most receptive – Expand resources, introducing techniques to other parts of the organization – Find high-visibility, high-impact projects, then expand to cover all projects

Table 4.3 Obstacles in institutionalizing the usability function

Step	Activities	Tips and obstacles
Institutionalization	– Integrate the new method with the development organization's standard methodology – Get the new method into both the formal, documented methodology and into the actual, living, practiced methodology	– Many organizations go successfully from stage one to stage two and never get to stage three – Some organizations simply stay in phase two, with usability having an impact on certain projects but never becoming an institutionalized part of the overall development process – Most organizations fail to be strategic in phase three

tional efforts to failure and the personnel to a great deal of professional frustration. In particular, the two first steps – promotion and implementation – are often neglected and done ad hoc even though they are critical prerequisite steps for successful institutionalization.

In the first step, called promotion, the main focus is to influence people while identifying champions or motivators (Table 4.1). It is important at this step to make sure that the management staff share the same understanding about the new usability engineering technology and that they are committed to providing the necessary resources to move into the next phase. Having an influential internal advocate at the management level virtually guarantees such a commitment.

The second step, called implementation, consists of influencing the project and product. In this step, the new method will be practiced in a specific project or product (Table 4.2). This step requires that the manager in charge of the product or the project be one of the motivators who were identified in the previous step. The motivator should be an engineer and not a visionary.

The last step, institutionalization aims to transform the new technology or method to become a standard or institutionalized part of the way the whole organization does business, to develop the whole product line and to ensure quality (Table 4.3).

4.2 On the Development of Adoption-Centric Usability Methods

A multiperspective approach is required to facilitate a faster and more systematic adoption of the existing UE techniques in the mainstream software development processes. As indicated in Fig. 4.1, a potential solution can be found at the intersection of the fields of usability engineering, empirical software engineering and organizational learning.

In the field of usability engineering, few studies exist on the relationships between project constraints, failures and the perceived benefits of specific UE techniques. In fact – similar to software engineering – many UE frameworks and methods lack any form of assessment or empirical evidence regarding the cost-effectiveness of usability. The data delivered by such studies are critical for evaluating why, when and how a method is suitable with respect to project characteristics such as software type, domain, interaction technology and the degree of impact of system defects.

Empirical evidence can be used to support decision-making in selecting a subset of UE techniques for the most prominent project settings in an organization. Data on the usability of UE techniques from the point of view of project teams can help to improve the acceptance of the UE approach and to establish UE techniques in the overall development process.

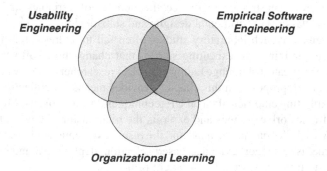

Fig. 4.1 Intersection of disciplines

From the organizational perspective, UE techniques have to be assessed as an organizational learning task. The term "organizational learning" has been discussed from the perspectives of fields as diverse as management science, psychology, sociology, and, more recently, information systems. However, a widely accepted model or even a consistent definition of organizational learning is still missing.

The classical definition by Agyris describes organizational learning as a process of "detection and correction of errors" (Agyris and Schön, 1978). According to Agyris' definition, an organizational learning system is the "ecological system of factors that facilitate or inhibit the learning activities of individuals".

This definition has been updated by more recent interpretations of organizational learning. Newer approaches view organizational learning as a process of knowledge acquisition, information interpretation and distribution (Huber, 1995) with the goal of having this knowledge being to modify the behavior of organizations (Garvin, 1993). The knowledge is acquired through experimentation, observation and analysis of both successes and failures (McGill et al., 1992).

This updated definition can be applied to studying the adoption of UE methods in software development organizations. Knowledge about UE techniques should be collected and disseminated in software development organizations to make the UE techniques accessible and easy to use for software engineering teams.

The emerging field of empirical software engineering also provides frameworks for conducting software engineering experiments to assess, compare and support decision-making regarding the usefulness, accuracy and adaptability of software engineering techniques (Basili et al., 1999). The most rigorous stream of this research interprets software engineering as a laboratory science.

According to this new research stream, software engineering techniques should be studied by using experimental designs and research methods similar to the controlled experiments conducted in classical disciplines such as physics, chemistry, usability engineering and HCI research.

However, such an approach to empirical software engineering suffers from several basic problems including measurement obstacles, difficulties in replicating experiments and the economical infeasibility of conducting controlled experiments in industrial settings (Juristo and Moreno, 2001). Controlled experiments are conducted almost exclusively in labs, for research purposes. The scope of the experiments is severely constrained to reduce the number of variables and allow the application of classical experimental designs and statistical tests.

Critics argue that such laboratory studies often fail to address significant problems and that "defining and executing studies that change how software development is done the greatest challenge facing empirical researchers" (Perry et al., 2000).

The framework proposed in this chapter provides means for collecting, accumulating and exploiting empirical data on UE techniques during projects. Moreover, the envisioned framework examines and exploits the relationships between the criteria for assessing usability on the one hand and the respective contexts of use on the other hand. The goal is to support evidence-based selection, deployment and evolution of UE methods in future software development projects.

4.3 Difficulties of Building an Empirical Driven Adoption Method

Several surveys on information system methodology research indicate that, in most cases, empirical studies of the effects of proposed techniques are largely missing. One consequence of this gap is that researchers kept proposing "new" engineering methodologies that, in essence, had already been built – they varied primarily in the names chosen for constructs (Smith and March, 1995). This uncertainty about the constructs proposed – mainly caused by a lack of empirical evaluation – leads to problems for both researchers and practitioners.

For researchers, the question of how to optimally integrate UE techniques into the software development lifecycle generally degenerates into "religious wars" (Paterno, 2002). A current prominent example is the dispute between the scenario-based and task-based camps (Benyon and Macaulay, 2002); (Carey, 2002); (Carrol, 2002); (Paterno, 2002). Such disputes are largely caused by a lack of empirical evidence to support a decision. Based on which data should a researcher improve or extend a UE technique if empirical data are not available on its advantages and drawbacks?

For practitioners, the situation is even worse. Based on which criteria should a project manager, usability engineer or user interface software developer select an approach, methodology, technique, best practice, pattern or guideline? If there is no empirical data to justify the selection of a technique, then why should anyone care about these techniques at all?

A look at software engineering where similar problems exist provides no ad hoc solutions to this problem. "No matter which software engineering methods are selected for a particular project, in almost all cases, there is little hard evidence backing up these decisions, and their costs and benefits are rarely understood" (Perry et al., 2000). In fact, the fundamental factors and mechanisms that drive the costs and benefits of software tools and methods are largely unknown (Basili et al., 1999). Therefore an Adoption-Centric Usability Engineering approach should provide means for incrementally building such a body of evidence. Without it, choosing a particular UE technique for a project becomes a random act.

In more mature scientific disciplines such as chemistry or physics, patterns of knowledge are built using the scientific principle of hypothesis building and hypothesis testing. These scientific principles are likewise necessary for examining UE techniques. However, it is initially unclear how to transfer these principles to examining the quality of UE techniques.

If we accept the scientific cycle of hypothesis building and hypothesis testing as a framework for building a pattern of knowledge of UE techniques, we first have to know which questions we want to ask. Each UE technique contains an implicit hypothesis that the technique is an appropriate means for solving a specific problem in the engineering of interactive systems.

Finding an appropriate experimental setting for such experiments continues to be a problem. A number of settings are possible for conducting experiments with

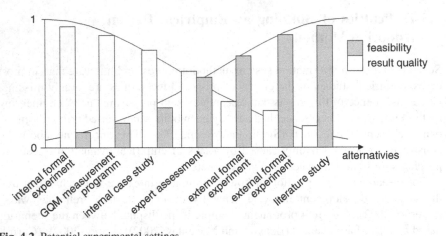

Fig. 4.2 Potential experimental settings

software engineering techniques (Basili et al., 1999); (Houdek, 1999); (Kitchenham, 1996); (Zelkowitz and Wallace, 1998). Houdek differentiates between internal formal experiments, internal case studies, expert assessments, external formal experiment, external case studies and literature studies (see Fig. 4.2).

According to this classification, "external" means that the respective study is conducted in a non-industrial environment, for example as part of a university course. Houdek ranks these alternatives according to the quality of results generated by the studies and their feasibility. According to Houdek's classification, internal formal experiments yield an optimal quality of results, but are almost impossible to conduct in most industrial software engineering settings (Houdek, 1999). At the other extreme, external case studies are rather easy to handle for the industry partner, but it is hard to interpret them and transfer the conclusions back to an industrial setting.

According to Houdek's classification, internal case studies and expert assessments are a good compromise between quality of results and feasibility. A project P in which a UE technique U is applied must be interpreted as an experiment to examine the quality of the technique under the conditions of project P.

But it still remains unclear how to measure the quality of UE techniques. The principles of natural science cannot be directly carried over to the study of engineering methods. Recently, it has been argued that research on the engineering of software systems needs to adopt research methods of the social sciences. This stream of software engineering research is interested in learning about the engineering of systems by observing the complex social settings existing in software engineering projects (Lofland and Lofland, 1995). Recent results of this research stream indicate that the organizational context where the interaction among humans takes place is the critical factor that determines the quality and effectiveness of the results.

A less technology-focused study of the quality of engineering methods can also be motivated from a philosophy of science point of view. Techniques for developing interactive software systems clearly belong to the domain of design science (Pinheiro da Silva and Paton, 2001); (Simon, 1981); (Smith and March, 1995).

While the aim of natural science is to understand and explain phenomena, the aim of design science is to create things that serve human purposes and develop ways to achieve human goals.

The utility principle yields important implications for measuring the quality of UE techniques. A prerequisite for the adoption of techniques is their acceptance by the people who are to use them. In the social sciences, various models exist for measuring acceptance. The technology acceptance model (TAM) represents one of the most prominent theoretical contributions to the understanding of acceptance behaviors (Davis et al., 1989); (Robey, 1996).

TAM aims to understand and predict the usage of computer systems (Davis, 1986). TAM postulates that tool acceptance can be predicted by measuring two dimensions: the perceived usefulness and the perceived ease-of-use of a software system.

TAM is based on fundamental theories of psychology such as the theory of reasoned action (TRA) (Fishbein and Ajzen, 1975). TRA examines which factors determine consciously intended behaviors. According to TRA, a person's performance of a specified behavior is determined by two central factors:

- First, by the person's attitude toward the behavior (A)
- And second, by the subjective norm (SN): the social pressure put on the person to perform the behavior

Attitude and subjective norm together form the behavioral intention (BI) of the person to perform the behavior.

TRA is a widely studied and accepted model of social psychology (see [Sheppard et al., 1988] for a review). The theory of reasoned action is depicted in Fig. 4.3.

Davis' technology acceptance model uses TRA as a theoretical basis and adapts it to the specific case of technology acceptance. Davis proposes that the attitude toward using an information system is influenced by two determinants: the perceived usefulness (PU) and the perceived ease-of-use (PEU) of a system.

The **perceived usefulness** of the system expresses the "subjective probability that using a specific application system will increase (the user's) job performance within an organizational context", i.e. it is a measure for the perceived utility of the system.

The **perceived ease-of-use** is the main factor that influences the acceptance of a system. Davis defines perceived ease-of-use as "the degree to which the user expects the target system to be free of effort", i.e. it is a measure for the usability of a system.

Together, perceived ease-of-use and perceived usefulness constitute the person's attitude toward using a system. The attitude (A) and the perceived ease-of-use (PEU) influence the behavioral intention (BI) which can be used to predict the actual use of the system. The technology acceptance model (TAM) is depicted in Fig. 4.4.

The postulated effects of perceived usefulness and perceived ease-of-use on technology acceptance have been confirmed by a large number of studies, and TAM is perceived as one of the most influential models for examining technology acceptance (Davis et al., 1989); (Robey, 1996).

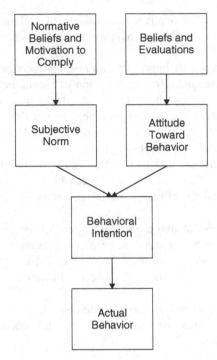

Fig. 4.3 Theory of reasoned action

There have been numerous reports on the acceptance failure of software engineering process improvement programs; we believe that the broader findings on acceptance of technology could shed some light on the acceptance of development methods (Riemenschneider et al., 2000). For example, many metrics techniques failed to become established, not because of inferior statistical models but because they were perceived by project staff as too tedious and time-consuming compared to the perceived benefits (Goldenson et al., 1999); (Niessink and Van Vliet, 1999); (Rosenberg and Hyatt, 1996). Measuring the quality of a method in terms of its acceptance by practitioners is a basis for improving the method and an opportunity for advancing the field.

An adoption-centric approach to the introduction and establishment of usability engineering within an organization needs a credible empirical base in order for practitioners to make decisions on the deployment of UE techniques. Such an empirical base can be incrementally constructed by conducting experiments in which the acceptance of methods is measured.

Software engineering projects in which UE techniques are deployed can be understood as experiments with UE techniques. The experiments consist of applying a UE technique U under the conditions S defined by the constraints of a project P. The acceptance of the UE technique can be measured in terms of perceived usefulness PU and perceived ease-of-use PEU as perceived by the project team T. After conducting such an experiment, we have some evidence to either support or

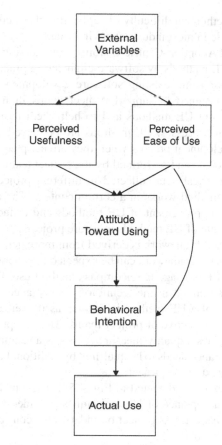

Fig. 4.4 Technology acceptance model

reject the deployment of the technique U under similar conditions S' in a future project P'.

4.4 Adoption-Centric Usability Engineering – Key Principles

In mature sciences, evidence can be strengthened by replicating the experiment. The most common type of replication is a repetition of the experiment under the same conditions S as in the initial experiment. The results of each replication are aggregated to get stronger conclusions than from the single observations. However, when we choose real industrial software development projects as a target for replication, this replication approach becomes problematic. Replication in the classical sense would mean to have the same project team with the same knowledge and experience, to develop the same system, with the same time constraints. In addition to the extreme methodical difficulty of replicating these conditions, the goal is economically infeasible in most industrial environments.

The overall goal of Adoption-Centric Usability Engineering (ACUE) is to facilitate the adoption of UE methods by software engineering practitioners and thereby improve their integration into existing software development methodologies and practices. ACUE is designed to support project teams in institutionalizing this abstract knowledge about UE methods and to help them transfer this knowledge into their development processes. UE methods are perceived as integrated into an existing software development process when they are adopted by the project team, i.e. when they are accepted and performed by the project team.

ACUE exploits empirical data collected in different projects to yield stronger evidence on how the method works in a certain context. The data form an empirical base to guide the improvement of UE methods and to facilitate the informed selection and deployment of UE methods in future projects.

Because the proposed framework is derived from more general theories of motivated human behavior, the framework can be expected to generalize to a large extent beyond the domain of tool usage to encompass method use. Building on the concept of acceptance as defined in the technology acceptance model (Davis et al., 1989), the acceptance of a UE method is defined as its perceived usefulness and ease-of-use from the perspective of project teams. The acceptance of UE methods by project teams provides a quality measure to assess and improve their adoption. This measure of acceptance needs to be qualified by additional data that characterize the constraints or context of the project.

The ACUE meta-model is depicted in Fig. 4.5. It uses qualitative and quantitative feedback on the acceptance of UE techniques provided by project teams and accumulates this feedback across project boundaries for controlling and improving the adoption of UE activities.

First, models need to be defined for measuring the acceptance of UE methods and for characterizing the projects in which the UE methods are to be deployed. Next, UE methods need to be captured to form a pool of methods for potential deployment in software development projects. For each captured method, its intended context of use needs to be defined. Sources for potential UE methods are the various existing UE methodologies.

In the next step, a subset of UE methods is selected from the method pool for deployment in a project. The appropriateness of a method for a project is assessed based on two criteria. According to the first criterion, the characteristics of the methods to be deployed in a project should match the characteristics of the project. According to the second criterion, candidate methods should have accumulated a high level of acceptance via acceptance assessments by project teams in previous projects.

In the next step, the project team is supported in mapping the selected methods onto the overall software development process and is guided in deploying the methods. After deployment of each selected method, the project team assesses the acceptance of the method.

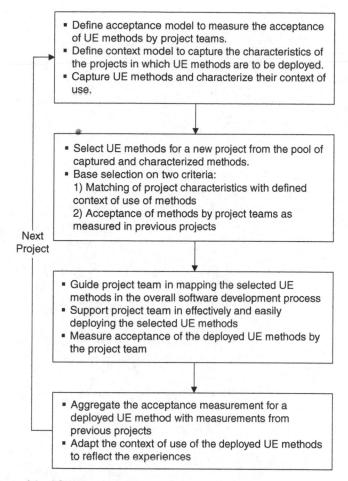

Fig. 4.5 Steps of the ACUE meta-model

Finally, the assessment results for each method are aggregated with the assessment results of previous projects. Also the context of use of each method is adapted to reflect new experiences with characteristics of projects which contribute to the acceptance or rejection of a method. This cycle is repeated for each new project, in order to accumulate empirical data about the acceptance of specific usability engineering methods and their context of use.

Chapter 5
ACUE Architecture and Components

This chapter details Adoption-Centric Usability Engineering (ACUE) ingredients including method kits, Usability Engineering Experience Packages (USEPacks), context profiles and acceptance models. These key components and their interrelation are described at a conceptual level. A necessary step toward the operationalization of the framework is the further elaboration and formalization of the models and computational steps. The formalization is presented in the next chapter.

5.1 UE Method Kits

Within the ACUE approach, usability engineer (UE) method kits are proposed as a central concept for integrating usability engineering methods into software development processes. UE method kits are lightweight abstractions of usability engineering methodologies, and can be configured to the characteristics of a software development project. They facilitate a mapping of usability engineering methods onto software development processes via logical process phases, usability engineering activities and a model of the project context.

UE method kits are lightweight because they make minimal assumptions about the structure of the underlying software engineering process model practiced in a project. The only assumption is that in the overall software development process, a set of logical process phases are common to almost all engineering processes. Examples of such logical process phases are Project planning, Requirements development, Production of solutions, and Evaluation of system against requirements. As a starting point, the phases of a UE method kit are based on existing software engineering and usability engineering standards such as ISO/TC 159 Ergonomics (1999) and ISO-SPICE (1998).

A set of usability engineering activities is assigned to be performed in each logical process phase. The general activities of usability engineering are relatively undisputed. References for such activities are International Organization for Standardization (2000) and ISO/TC 159 Ergonomics (1999). Examples of usability engineering activities are "Identify user attributes" and "Define usability objectives".

A. Seffah, E. Metzker, *Adoption-centric Usability Engineering*,
DOI 10.1007/978-1-84800-019-3_5, © Springer-Verlag London Limited 2009

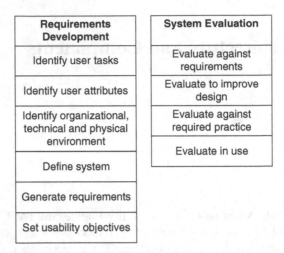

Requirements Development	System Evaluation
Identify user tasks	Evaluate against requirements
Identify user attributes	Evaluate to improve design
Identify organizational, technical and physical environment	Evaluate against required practice
Define system	Evaluate in use
Generate requirements	
Set usability objectives	

Fig. 5.1 Two process phases of a sample UE method kit

Figure 5.1 illustrates two process phases from a sample UE method kit. It shows the two logical process phases "requirements development" and "system evaluation" together with a set of usability engineering activities for each phase. These phases are just an excerpt of a sample method kit. The goal of the method kit concept is not to describe one specific methodology. Activities and phases can be freely selected to form different method kits.

By relying on logical process phases and associated usability engineering activities, UE method kits consciously abstract from existing UE lifecycle models. This enables project team members, who are the actual users of UE method kits, to easily map UE process activities onto their software development process.

The most obvious abstraction is that the process phases in this model do not include the rigorous temporal dependencies that are portrayed in lifecycle models by linking their activities with arrows. The goals can be arranged to form many different lifecycles, and the exact sequence and the iterative paths depend on the dynamics of the project. It is therefore difficult and possibly even confusing to create a single visualization that defines how the usability engineering activities of a UE method kit are linked.

Another abstraction introduced by UE method kits is the conceptual separation of usability engineering activities from the specific UE methods that employ these activities. Most existing UE methodologies show a static, monolithic mapping between activities and UE methods. UE method kits introduce an experience-based, context-sensitive mapping of UE methods to usability engineering activities. To facilitate the project-specific mapping of UE methods to usability engineering activities, the ACUE framework uses the concepts of a project context profile and a usability engineering experience package (USEPack) (Metzker and Reiterer, 2002).

Figure 5.2 provides a structural overview of the UE method kit concept. For simple "has a" relationships between entities, the relationship attribute is omitted. Concepts that are further decomposed and explained in this section are marked in grey.

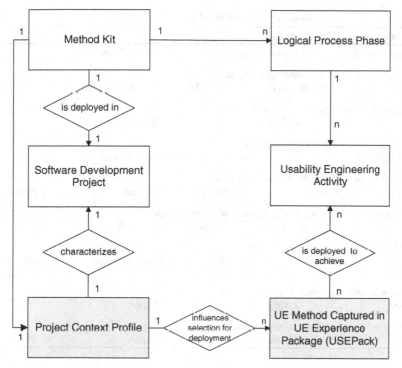

Fig. 5.2 Conceptual structure of a UE method kit

Software engineering projects provide the setting for deploying and studying the quality of usability engineering methods and best practices, which in turn are captured in USEPacks and structured via method kits.

5.2 Project Context Profile

Each project has characteristics that influence the perceived usefulness and ease-of-use of a UE technique. For example, some UE evaluation techniques are highly useful when assessing Graphical User Interface(GUI)-based software systems, but are of low value when assessing multimodal user interfaces. Other project characteristics that can influence the perceived usefulness and ease-of-use of UE techniques are the experience of the project team in the domain and the spatial distribution of the project team. From an experimentation point of view, these project characteristics are the parameters of the experiment.

The characteristics of a given project are captured in a project context profile. Each project context profile consists of a set of context factors. The potential values of a context factor are described by its context factor characteristics. The state of a project context factor characteristic indicates whether the characteristic applies to the project in which the associated method kit is to be deployed. The ACUE

Table 5.1 An example of project context profile

C1: Criticality of usability defects for users				
Loss of comfort	Loss of money		Loss of lives	
C2: Complexity of human–computer interaction				
Command-line	Form-based	GUI	Multimodal	
C3: Complexity of domain				
Low	Medium		High	
C4: Initial definition of the product goal				
Poorly defined	Fairly defined		Well defined	
C5: Maturity of software development process				
Initial	Repeatable	Defined	Managed	Optimizing
C6: Ratio of number of developers/number of usability experts				
0	11–20	6–10	1–5	
C7: Spatial distribution of project team				
Same room	Same floor	Same site	Same time zone	Different time zones
C8: Project team experience in product domain				
Novice	Qualified		Expert	
C9: Project team experience in application type				
Novice	Qualified		Expert	

framework provides no recommendations on specific context factors or on how many should be used. These properties depend on practical considerations and require empirical investigation.

Table 5.1 shows a context profile, which consists of nine context factors, C1–C9. Below each context factor, its characteristics are displayed. Dark grey shading indicates that the respective characteristic does not apply to the project in which the corresponding method kit is to be deployed. White shading indicates that the respective context characteristic correctly describes a property of the project in which the corresponding method kit is to be deployed. For example, context factor C1 describes the fact that usability defects of the product to be developed will in the worst case lead to a loss of comfort for the user. Context factor C6 indicates that there is not more than 1 usability expert available for 20 developers.

5.3 USEPacks: Knowledge About UE Methods

As already mentioned, USEPacks provide knowledge about UE methods and best practices. This knowledge is required to perform the usability engineering activities defined in a method kit. USEPacks are used to capture and evolve context-specific usability engineering knowledge. They can be used to describe well-defined UE techniques as well as new UE best practices that have been invented by project teams during a project.

USEPacks are based on the idea of experience packages (Basili et al., 1994). However, USEPacks extend this approach by using semi-formal concepts for the evaluation and evolution of the captured knowledge.

The structure of a USEPack is illustrated in Fig. 5.3. A USEPack consists of:

- A structured textual description
- A set of reusable artifacts
- A semi-formal model – the USEPack context profile – which describes factors that contributed to the acceptance or rejection of the USEPack in previous projects and
- An acceptance profile as a measure for the acceptance of the USEPack by project teams

Below, each section of a USEPack is described in detail and illustrated with an example. The example is based on the streamlined cognitive walkthrough method described by Spencer (Spencer, 2000). In his article, Spencer describes the problems associated with applying the original cognitive walkthrough method (Polson et al., 1992) in a large software development organization. The experiences led Spencer to the development of the streamlined cognitive walkthrough method,

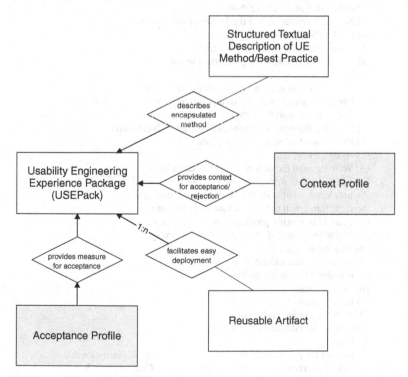

Fig. 5.3 Conceptual structure of a USEPack

which significantly improved the practicality of the original approach and its acceptance by development teams.

5.3.1 USEPack Textual Description

Table 5.2 shows the textual description part of the USEPack that encapsulates the "streamlined cognitive walkthrough" method developed by Spencer, together with a list of artifacts. The textual description explains the goals of the method or best

Table 5.2 Example of the textual description of a USEPack

Title: Streamlined Cognitive Walkthrough (SCW)	
Abstract: The SCW is an optimized UI inspection method that should be applied to counteract the social constraints of classical UI inspection methods. For this purpose the SCW provides a set of ground rules and steps. Description: Ground rules: – No design discussions during an SCW – No defending of a design – No debating of cognitive theory – The usability specialist is the leader of the session Steps of an SCW: (1) Define inputs to the walkthrough (a) Identify user tasks to be performed in the walkthrough (b) Identify action sequences for completing the task (c) Create a paper-based/electronic implementation of the interface (2) Convene the walkthrough (a) Describe the goals and non-goals of the walkthrough (b) Post ground rules in a visible place (c) Assign roles (3) Walk through the action sequences of each task (a) Tell a credible story for these two questions: Will the user know what to do at this step? If the user does the right thing, will they know that they did the right thing, and are making progress toward their goal? (b) Maintain control of the cognitive walkthrough, enforce the ground rules (4) Record critical information (a) Possible learnability problems (b) Design ideas (c) Design gaps (d) Problems in the task analysis (5) Revise the interface to fix the problems	
Artifacts:	
Heuristics for performing an SCW	SCW heuristics.doc
Template for recording critical information	Critical info. doc
Original SCW paper by Spencer	CHI00_Spencer.pdf

practice encapsulated in the USEPack and how it is applied in practice. The textual description is decomposed into the "title", "abstract" and "description" fields.

5.3.2 USEPack Reusable Artifacts

To facilitate ad hoc performance of the method by engineering teams, each USEPack contains a set of reusable artifacts. Artifacts are composed of reusable templates and examples of work products. Examples of artifacts include questionnaires for usability tests, checklists for user task analysis, and templates for capturing usability goals.

5.3.3 USEPack Context Profile

While the textual description and artifacts explain why and how a USEPack should be deployed, the USEPack context profile formally relates the USEPack to a project context. The USEPack context profile S^U describes under which conditions the method or best practice described in a USEPack was accepted or rejected by project teams. Analogously to a *project* context profile, a *USEPack* context profile consists of a set of context factors. USEPack context profiles and project context profiles share the same set of context characteristics. This shared set is called the context model.

Table 5.3 shows an example of a USEPack context profile. A background shade of dark grey indicates that the USEPack was largely rejected by project teams in projects that shared this characteristic. A background shade of light grey indicates that not enough data is available to support the rejection or acceptance of the USEPack by the project team in projects that shared this characteristic. A background shade of white indicates that the USEPack was largely accepted by the project team in projects that shared this characteristic. Chapter 6 describes how expressions such as "largely rejected" and "largely accepted" are quantified.

5.3.4 Acceptance Model

An acceptance model Q is used to measure the acceptance of a USEPack by the project team. The acceptance model provides a set of acceptance factors and a set of items and scales, which are used to measure the required data for each acceptance factor. The project team assesses the USEPack based on the questions defined in the acceptance model. The acceptance profile of the USEPack aggregates the results of multiple assessments.

Each item has a rating scale. On the rating scales provided in the example, the project team can decide if it totally agrees (TA), agrees (T), disagrees (D), totally disagrees (TD) or neither (N) agrees nor disagrees with the statement in the item. The box highlighted in grey indicates which rating has been assigned to that acceptance factor by the acceptance model Q.

Table 5.3 Example of a USEPack context profile

C1: Criticality of usability defects for users				
Loss of comfort	Loss of money	Loss of lives		

C2: Complexity of human–computer interaction

Command-line	Form-based	GUI	Multimodal	

C3: Complexity of domain

Low	Medium	High		

C4: Initial definition of the product goal

Poorly defined	Fairly defined	Well defined		

C5: Maturity of software development process

Initial	Repeatable	Defined	Managed	Optimizing

C6: Ratio of #Number of developers/#Usability experts

0	11–20	6–10	1–5	

C7: Spatial distribution of project team

Same room	Same floor	Same site	Same time zone	Different time zones

C8: Project team experience in product domain

Novice	Qualified	Expert		

C9: Project team experience in application type

Novice	Qualified	Expert		

Table 5.4 shows the acceptance profile measuring the acceptance factor "perceived ease-of-use" and the associated items h1.1–h1.6. Table 5.5 shows the acceptance profile measuring the acceptance factor "perceived usefulness" and the associated items h2.1–h2.6. The acceptance factors, items and rating scales are based on Davis' technology acceptance model (Davis, 1986). The two examples illustrate how different acceptance factors can have different measurement factors.

Table 5.4 Example of a USEPack acceptance profile

q1: Perceived ease-of-use

h1.1: Learning to apply this USEPack is easy for the project team
1(TA)   2(A)   3(N)   4(D)   5(TD)

h1.2: The project team finds the USEPack to be compatible with its way of working
1(TA)   2(A)   3(N)   4(D)   5(TD)

h1.3: The project team finds it easy to get the required results by applying this USEPack.
1(TA)   2(A)   3(N)   4(D)   5(TD)

h1.4: It is easy for the project team to become skillful in deploying this USEPack.
1(TA)   2(A)   3(N)   4(D)   5(TD)

h1.5: The USEPack is easy to use.
1(TA)   2(A)   3(N)   4(D)   5(TD)

h1.6: The deployment of this USEPack is clear and understandable.
1(TA)   2(A)   3(N)   4(D)   5(TD)

Table 5.5 Example of USEPack acceptance profile (continued)

q2: Perceived usefulness

h2.1: Using this USEPack improves the job performance of the project team.
1(TA) 2(A) 3(N) 4(D) 5(TD)

h2.2: Using this USEPack in our project enables the project team to accomplish tasks more
   quickly.
1(TA) 2(A) 3(N) 4(D) 5(TD)

h2.3: The project team finds this USEPack useful.
1(TA) 2(A) 3(N) 4(D) 5(TD)

h2.4: Using this USEPack in the project increase the productivity of the project team.
1(TA) 2(A) 3(N) 4(D) 5(TD)

h2.5: Using this USEPack enhances the project team's effectiveness in the job.
1(TA) 2(A) 3(N) 4(D) 5(TD)

h2.6: Using this USEPack makes the development task easier for the project team.
1(TA) 2(A) 3(N) 4(D) 5(TD)

Each rating in a USEPack acceptance profile is the result of a calculation performed by the acceptance model Q on acceptance results from a number of projects.
For example in Tables 5.4 and 5.5, the measurement factor h1.4 examines whether
project teams find it easy to get the required results by applying the USEPack. The

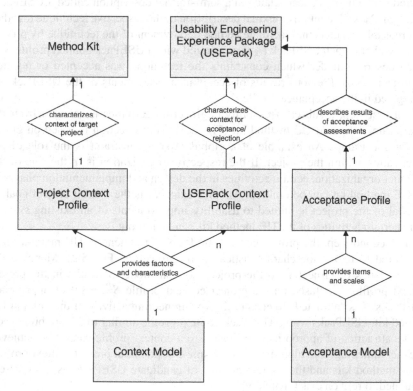

Fig. 5.4 Relation of context and acceptance models to method kits and USEPacks

context profile indicates that the average assessment of this item by project teams is in total agreement with the statement.

From an experimentation point of view, the quality factors $q_1, \ldots, q_2$ are the response variables of experiments on the acceptance of UE methods. Each value v_i assigned to a quality factor q_i during the assessment of the acceptance of a USEPack is an observation of the experiment.

5.3.5 Context Model vs. Context Profile

Figure 5.4 illustrates the relationships between context models and context profiles as well as between acceptance models and acceptance profiles.

5.4 Configuration of a Method Kit to a Specific Project

Figure 5.5 portrays the key stages for configuring a default method kit. According to Adoption-Centric Usability Engineering, the usability engineering process is not static and monolithic. Instead it consists of a pool of defined UE methods. Each method of the pool is encapsulated in a semi-formal description called a USEPack. Each USEPack U_k contains a textual description of the respective technique together with reusable artifacts that facilitate ad hoc deployment of the technique by project team members. Each USEPack U_k is associated with a USEPack context profile S^{U_k}, which describes under which constraints the technique was accepted or rejected by project teams. Previous results of acceptance assessments of the USEPack are aggregated in the acceptance profile.

In a first step, a subset of usability engineering activities is selected from the generic, unconfigured UE method kit (Fig. 5.5). This selection is based on global project constraints. An example of a global project constraint is the role of the organization within the project. If the respective organization is in the role of the customer organization, certain activities in the design and implementation phases of the UE method kit can be omitted. Another example is the overall project goal. If the goal of the project is limited to usability improvements of an existing system, again certain activities of the UE method kit can be left out.

In a second step, the project context model S of the generic UE method kit is configured to reflect the characteristics of the project P (Fig. 5.2). Mapping the characteristics of project P to the project context model S results in the project context profile S^P. Based on the project context profile S^P, a set of appropriate USEPacks U is "attracted" to each usability engineering activity of the tailored UE method kit. USEPacks with a USEPack context profile similar to S^P are preferred.

The attraction of appropriate USEPacks to a context profile cannot be achieved by exact matching. The high-dimensional space of potential project context profiles of the method kits and the context profiles of candidate USEPacks is too sparsely populated to rely on exact matching.

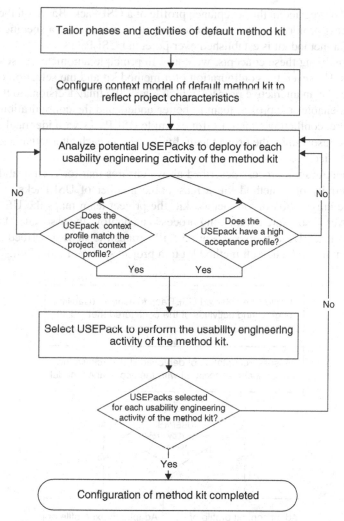

Fig. 5.5 Steps for configuring a default method kit

Instead of an exact matching process, a formula is used to select USEPacks based on similarity between the given project context profile and USEPack context profiles. The project context profile encodes the constraints of the projects in which a method kit is to be deployed. The USEPacks context profiles encode which constraints applied to the projects in which the USEPack was accepted or rejected by the project team.

In addition to matching the project context profile, the other criterion for the project team to select appropriate USEPacks is the accumulated assessment result of a USEPack. In Fig. 5.5, this corresponds to the diamond with the text "Does the USEPack have a high acceptance profile?" As described above, previous assessment results are aggregated in the acceptance profile of a USEPack. Based on the similarity of context profiles and the acceptance profile, a ranking for a specific usability activity of a method kit is established over potential USEPacks.

By formalizing these concepts, we could in principle automate the selection of USEPacks. However, the configuration of a method kit and the selection of USEPacks should be an interactive process, which leaves the final decisions to the project team. This enables the project team to better understand the configuration process. Furthermore, conflicting situations, for example USEPacks with identical rankings, can best be resolved by the project team by inspecting each alternative and making a conscious decision.

The configuration process described above ensures that for each usability engineering activity of a method kit, a reasonable number of USEPacks is selected. After the configuration of the method kit, the project team maps the UE activities onto the overall software engineering process and deploys the associated USEPacks to perform these UE activities. Figure 5.5 illustrates the steps described above for the configuration of a default method kit to a project specific method kit.

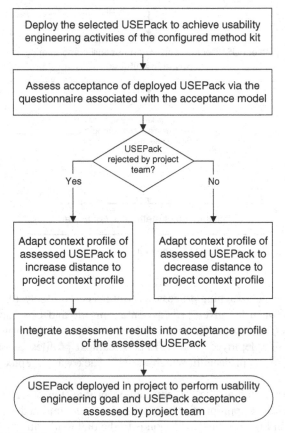

Fig. 5.6 Steps of the USEPack assessment process

5.5 USEPack Assessment

The project team performs the usability engineering methods and best practices specified in the USEPacks. After completion of major project phases or in post mortem sessions (Birk et al., 2002), the project team assesses the acceptance of each deployed USEPack by using the questionnaire associated with the acceptance model. Figure 5.6 shows the overall assessment and adaptation process of the USEPacks.

One assessment of a USEPack by a project team provides two data sets for the adaptation of the USEPack: first, the acceptance assessment that indicates the team's rating of each acceptance factor, and second, the context profile of the method kit, which describes the characteristics of the project in which the USEPack was deployed.

Based on the assessment, the USEPack context profile S^{U_k} of each USEPack deployed in the project is adapted. For USEPacks with a negative assessment, the USEPack context profile is adapted to have a lower probability of being selected in subsequent projects P' with a similar project context $S^{P'}$. For USEPacks with a positive assessment, the USEPack context profile is adapted to have a higher probability of being selected in subsequent projects P' with a similar project context $S^{P'}$.

By applying this approach, project team feedback on the acceptance of usability engineering techniques is accumulated across projects. After a number of iterations, the USEPack context profile becomes a description of the optimal context of use of the method captured in the USEPack U_k. Through this accumulation, it is possible to arrive at stronger conclusions about the perceived usefulness and ease-of-use of specific UE methods in defined contexts.

Chapter 6
ACUE Formal Description

The previous chapter identified the principles of Adoption-Centric Usability Engineering as well as the basic elements of the framework such as method kits, Usability Engineering Experience Packages (USEPacks), context profiles and acceptance models. A necessary step toward the operationalization of the framework is the further elaboration and formalization of the models and computational steps of the framework. In this chapter the mathematical methods for computationally handling the constructs of Adoption-Centric Usability Engineering are developed. The theories that are selected as a basis for this purpose are multi-criteria decision-making (Triantaphyllou, 2000) and fuzzy sets (Zadeh, 1965). Fuzzy sets are used to formalize the concept of context profiles to allow for quantifying the acceptance or rejection of USEPacks in a certain context. Multi-criteria decision-making is used as a basis to formulate an algorithm for selecting appropriate USEPacks for a given project context profile. Furthermore, an algorithm for adapting USEPack context profiles based on acceptance assessments of project teams is developed. This algorithm facilitates to incrementally accumulate and exploit data gathered in different projects on factors that contribute to the acceptance or rejection of usability engineer (UE) methods. The algorithm allows fusing information collected in different projects to yield stronger conclusions about the acceptance of specific UE methods than those available from each individual project. At the end of this chapter, potential alternatives for the formalisms used are briefly discussed and the rational for the formalisms used is described.

6.1 Foundations for ACUE Formalization

In this section the concepts of the theory of fuzzy subsets and multi-criteria decision-making are briefly introduced. They are used to formalize the concepts of Adoption-Centric Usability Engineering. The formalization facilitates the comparison of project context profiles and USEPack context profiles and thereby enables the selection of appropriate methods for the deployment in a given project.

A. Seffah, E. Metzker, *Adoption-centric Usability Engineering*,
DOI 10.1007/978-1-84800-019-3_6, © Springer-Verlag London Limited 2009

6.1.1 Fuzzy Sets

Fuzzy sets were introduced by Zadeh as a generalization of conventional set theory
to represent the vagueness of concepts in practical situations (Zadeh, 1965).

Conventional sets or Cantor sets are defined as any collection of objects which
can be treated as a whole. A set $A = \{a_0, a_1, \ldots, a_n\}$ can be specified by its members that characterize a set completely. An example of a conventional set is "the
set of non-negative integers smaller than four". This set is specified by the list of
members $A = \{0, 1, 2, 3\}$.

According to Zadeh, many sets that occur in everyday life cannot be expressed
by using crisp decisions regarding the membership of their items. They require more
than an "either"-or criterion for describing the membership of their items. A classical example for such sets is the set of "young people". While a child of two years
is clearly a member of this set and a person aged 100 will not be a member of
this set, the membership of people at the age of 20, 30 or 40 is more ambiguous.
Zadeh proposed a grade of membership such that the transition from membership to
non-membership is gradual rather than abrupt. Thus a fuzzy set is described by the
grade of membership $\mu(x) \in [0, 1]$ of all its members x. The grade of membership
of an item is a real number between zero and one. The higher this number is, the
higher is the degree of membership of the item.

It should be noted that Zadeh does not give a formal basis for how to determine
the grade of membership. The grade of membership is a precise but subjective measure that depends on the context. For example, the membership of a 50 year old in
the set of "young people" depends on one's own view.

According to Zadeh the concept of a fuzzy set can be defined as follows:

Let E be a finite set, and let x be an Element of E. A fuzzy set $\tilde{A}$ of E is a set of
ordered pairs:

$$\tilde{A} = \left\{ (x, \mu_{\tilde{A}}(x)) \right\} \ \forall x \in E$$

$\mu_{\tilde{A}}(x)$ Is the level or degree of membership of x in $\tilde{A}$. If $\mu_{\tilde{A}}(x)$ takes its values in a
set M we can write:

$$\mu_{\tilde{A}}(x) : x \rightarrow M \ \forall x \in E$$

$\mu_{\tilde{A}}(x)$ is called the membership characteristic function M is called the membership
set. E is called the support set. If $M = \{0, 1\}$ we have the case where $\tilde{A}$ is a non-
fuzzy set or ordinary set.

$$\mu_{\tilde{A}}(x)$$

Section 6.2 describes how fuzzy sets are used to model context factors of USEPack
and project context profiles.

6.1.2 Multi-Criteria Decision-Making

Multi-criteria decision-making (MCDM) is an approach that assists decision makers in evaluating alternatives. MCDM has a wide range of applications. In particular, it has been widely applied to strategic decision problems in business. The aim of multi-criteria decision analysis is to recommend an action, while several alternatives have to be evaluated in terms of many criteria.

According to (Kickert, 1978) the MCDM problem is usually described as follows: A MCDM problem is defined by a set of v alternatives $A = \{A_1, A_2, \ldots, A_v\}$, a set of n criteria $C = \{C_1, C_2, \ldots, C_n\}$ and a profile A_0. An alternative $A_k \in \{0, 1\}^n$ is an n-dimensional binary vector. The i-th element of this vector p_{ki} encodes whether the criterion C_i is fulfilled for this alternative or not. The goal is to find the alternative A_k, which optimally satisfies the requirements $(p_{01}, p_{02}, \ldots, p_{0n})$ given by the profile A_0.

Table 6.1 shows the constellation for finding an alternative A_k that matches the requirements defined by the profile A_0: The performance of alternative A_k when it is examined under criteria C_i is denoted $p_{ki} : A \times C \rightarrow \{0, 1\}$, i.e. the performance of alternative A_k to criterion C_i is either zero or one.

To find the alternative A_k that best matches the profile A_0 considering all n criteria C_i, the similarity of the corresponding n-dimensional binary vectors $(p_{01}, p_{02}, \ldots, p_{0n})$ and $(p_{k1}, p_{k2}, \ldots, p_{kn})$ is determined. The matching of alternative A_k and the profile A_0 is expressed by the rank q_k of alternative A_k. The rank of an alternative A_k when it is examined under all criteria $C_1, C_2, \ldots, C_n$ is denoted as q_k.

According to Kickert (1978) several methods are available to compute the rank q_k for an alternative A_k. Possible methods to determine the rank q_k are the vector product or the complimentary hamming distance. The vector product, for example, calculates the overlap of alternative A_k and the profile A_0, i.e. the vector product is a measure for the number of criteria of the profile A_0 satisfied by alternative A_k:

$$q_k = \frac{1}{n} \sum_{i-1}^{n} p_{0i} p_{ki}, q_k \in [0, 1]$$

Table 6.1 Criteria and alternatives in a MCDM problem

		Criteria				
		C_1	$\ldots$	C_i	$\ldots$	C_n
Profile	A_0	p_{01}	$\ldots$	p_{0i}	$\ldots$	p_{0n}
Alternatives	A_1	p_{11}	$\ldots$	p_{1i}	$\ldots$	p_{1n}
	$\vdots$	$\vdots$		$\vdots$		$\vdots$
	A_k	p_{k1}	$\ldots$	p_{ki}	$\ldots$	p_{kn}
	$\vdots$	$\vdots$		$\vdots$		$\vdots$
	A_v	p_{v1}	$\ldots$	p_{vi}	$\ldots$	p_{vn}

The rank has the value $q_k = 1$ if A_0 as well as A_k satisfy all n criteria and the rank has the value $q_k = 0$ if no criterion of A_0 is satisfied by A_k.

The complementary hamming distance is a measure for the number of criteria that A_0 has in common with alternative A_k.

$$q_k = 1 - \frac{1}{n} \sum_{i=1}^{n} |p_{0i} - p_{ki}|, q_k \in [0, 1]$$

The rank has the value $q_k = 1$ if all criteria of A0 are identical with the corresponding criteria of A_k: $p_{0i} = p_{ki} \forall 1 \leq i \leq n$. The rank has the value $q_k = 0$ if no criterion of A_0 is identical with the corresponding criterion of A_k: $p_{0i} \neq p_{ki} \forall 1 \leq i \leq n$.

In Section 6.1.4 the task of selecting appropriate USEPacks which match to the project context profile of a method kit is formulated as a MCDM problem and a measure for calculating the matching of project context factors and USEPack context factors is developed.

6.1.3 Modeling Context Profiles as Fuzzy Sets

In this section the concept of fuzzy sets introduced in Section 6.1 is applied to formally describe the structure of USEPack context profiles and project context profiles.

A context profile S^{U_k} of a USEPack U_k consists of a set of n context factors $\tilde{C}_i^{U_k}$ which form a fuzzy set. Each USEPack context factor consists of a set of w_i characteristics c_{ij}. The characteristic c_{ij} is identical for each USEPack context factor $\tilde{C}_i^{U_k}$ in all USEPack context profiles S^{U_k} and for each project context factor $\tilde{C}_i^P$ in all project context profiles S^P. Each USEPack context factor characteristic c_{ij} is associated with a value $\mu_{\tilde{C}_i^{U_k}}(c_{ij}) \in [0, 1]$ which can differ for each context factor $\tilde{C}_i^{U_k}$ in the USEPack context profiles. Correspondingly each characteristic c_{ij} of a project context factor $\tilde{C}_i^P$ is associated with a value $\mu_{\tilde{C}_i^P}(c_{ij})$ which can differ in each project context profile S^P.

Thus a USEPack context factor can be written as the fuzzy set $\tilde{C}_i^{U_k}$:

$$\tilde{C}_i^{U_k} = \left\{ (c_{i1}, \mu_{\tilde{C}_i^{U_k}}(c_{i1})), \ldots, (c_{iw_i}, \mu_{\tilde{C}_i^{U_k}}(c_{iw_i})) \right\}.$$

where w_i is the number of characteristics of the i-th context factor. Analogously a project context factor can be written as the fuzzy set $\tilde{C}_i^P$:

$$\tilde{C}_i^P = \left\{ (c_{i1}, \mu_{\tilde{C}_i^P}(c_{i1})), \ldots, (c_{iw_i}, \mu_{\tilde{C}_i^P}(c_{iw_i})) \right\}.$$

The semantic of a project context factor characteristic value-pair is defined as follows: The project context characteristic value $\mu_{\tilde{C}_i^P}(c_{ij})$ indicates whether the characteristic c_{ij} applies to the project P. A value $\mu_{\tilde{C}_i^P}(c_{ij}) = 0$ indicates that the context characteristic c_{ij} does not apply to the project P, i.e. that c_{ij} is not a correct characterization of project P. A value $\mu_{\tilde{C}_i^P}(c_{ij}) = 1$ indicates that the context characteristic c_{ij} does apply to the project P, i.e. that c_{ij} is a correct characterization of project P.

The semantic of a USEPack context factor characteristic value pair is defined as follows: The USEPack context factor characteristic value $\mu_{\tilde{C}_i^{U_k}}(c_{ij})$ is a measure for the acceptance which the USEPack U_k received in past projects P which shared the context factor characteristic c_{ij}, i.e. it is a measure for the acceptance which the USEPack U_k received in projects P where the context factor characteristic c_{ij} of the project context factor $\tilde{C}_i^P$ has the value $\mu_{\tilde{C}_i^P}(c_{ij}) = 1$.

The initial value of all USEPack context characteristics is $\mu_{\tilde{C}_i^{U_k}}(c_{ij}) = 0.5$ which expresses that nothing is known about the acceptance of USEPack U_k for projects P that share the context characteristic c_{ij}. Via USEPack assessments by project teams as described in Section 6.3, the initial value of $\mu_{\tilde{C}_i^{U_k}}(c_{ij})$ is adapted to reflect the degree of acceptance of a USEPack U_k in projects that share the context factor characteristic c_{ij}.

A value $\mu_{\tilde{C}_i^{U_k}}(c_{ij}) \to 0$ indicates that there was little support for the acceptance of USEPack U_k in projects that shared the context characteristic c_{ij}, i.e. the USEPack U_k was rejected by project teams in these projects. A value $\mu_{\tilde{C}_i^{U_k}}(c_{ij}) \to 1$ indicates that there was much support for the acceptance USEPack U_k in projects that shared the context characteristic c_{ij}.

Following the definitions given above a USEPack context profile S^{U_k} can be written as a set of fuzzy sets: $S^{U_k} = \{\tilde{C}_1^{U_k}, \tilde{C}_2^{U_k}, \ldots, \tilde{C}_n^{U_k}\}$. The characteristics of the USEPack context factor $\tilde{C}_i^{U_k}$ are represented by its support set $F_i^{U_k} = \{c_{11}, \ldots, c_{ij}, \ldots c_{iw_i}\}$. The union $F^U = \{c_{11}, \ldots, c_{ij}, \ldots c_{nw_n}\}$ of all support sets $F_i^{U_k} = \{c_{11}, \ldots, c_{ij}, \ldots c_{iw_i}\}$ contains all context factor characteristics of all USEPack context profiles S^{U_k}.

Analogously a project context profile S^P is defined as a set of fuzzy sets: $S^P = \{\tilde{C}_1^P, \tilde{C}_2^P, \ldots, \tilde{C}_n^P\}$. The characteristics of the project context factor $\tilde{C}_i^P$ are represented by its support set $F_i^P = \{c_{11}, \ldots, c_{ij}, \ldots c_{iw_i}\}$. The union $F^P = \{c_{11}, \ldots, c_{ij}, \ldots c_{nw_n}\}$ of all support sets $F_i^P = \{c_{11}, \ldots, c_{ij}, \ldots c_{iw_i}\}$ contains all context factor characteristics of the project context profile S^P. The support set $F = F^U = F^P$ is identical for all project context profiles of all projects P and all USEpack context profiles of all USEPacks U and is called the context model. The concepts explained above are illustrated in the following example:

Projects P can be characterized by the criticality of usability defects for the user of the systems developed in P. One potential effect of usability defects for a user can be the "loss of comfort". Errors in operating the climate control in a home environment for example will probably lead to a loss of comfort, if the room temperature cannot be adjusted as intended by the user. Another potential effect of usability defects for users can be the "loss of money". Usability defects in a stock portfolio management system for example can lead to a loss of money, if stocks are accidentally sold or bought. In the worst case usability defects which lead to operating errors can lead to a "loss of lives", e.g. usability defects which result in wrong decisions in operating driver assistance systems or plant control systems. These characteristics are captured in a context factor $\tilde{C}^P_{criticality}$ that is part of the project context profile S^P. $\tilde{C}^P_{criticality}$ has the following support set:

$$F_{criticality} = \{loss\ of\ comfort, loss\ of\ money, loss\ of\ lives\}.$$

To configure a method kit for the deployment of UE methods in project P, the context factors of the project context profile S^P need to be specified.

$$\tilde{C}^P_{criticality} = \{(loss\ of\ comfort, 0), (loss\ of\ money, 0), (loss\ of\ lives, 1)\}$$

A project context factor expresses that usability defects about a system developed in project P could lead to a loss of lives for the operators of the system. This could advocate the selection of more disciplined methods for the definition of usability goals and for usability inspections in project P to strongly assure the detection of usability defects. Such a project context factor leads to the preference of USEPacks U_k during the USEPack selection process that have a high context factor characteristic value

$$\mu_{\tilde{C}^P_{criticality}}(loss\ of\ lives).$$

A context factor $\tilde{C}^{U_k}_{criticality}$ as part of a USEPack context profile S^{U_k} of a USEPack U_k expresses, that the USEPack U_k reached a very high level of acceptance in projects that share the criticality of usability defects characteristic $c_{criticality3} = lives$, a medium level of acceptance in projects that share the criticality of usability defects characteristics $c_{criticality2} = money$ and a very low level of acceptance in projects that share the criticality of usability defects characteristic $c_{criticality1} = comfort$.

$$\tilde{C}^{U_k}_{criticality} = \{(comfort, 0.1), (money, 0.7), (lives, 0.9)\}$$

6.1.4 Context-Based USEPack Selection as a MCDM Problem

For method selection, the criteria are the n context factor characteristic sets $F^P_i = \{c_{i1}, \ldots, c_{iw_i}\}$ of the project context profile S^P of Project P. The profile is given by the project context profile S^P. The alternatives are the v USEPacks represented by their context profiles S^{U_k}. The level of appropriateness of the alternative S^{U_k} when it is examined under the characteristics F^P_i is described by the context factor characteristic values. For reasons of better readability the context factor characteristic values of a USEPack context factor $\tilde{C}^{U_k}_i$ are denoted as $s_{ki} = \mu_{\tilde{C}^{U_k}_i}(c_{i1}), \ldots, \mu_{\tilde{C}^{U_k}_i}(c_{iw_i})$. The context factor characteristic values of a project context factor $\tilde{C}^P_i$ are denoted as $s_{Pi} = \mu_{\tilde{C}^P_i}(c_{i1}), \ldots, \mu_{\tilde{C}^P_i}(c_{iw_i})$ where w_i is the number

Table 6.2 Project context factors and USEPack context profiles

		Project context factors					
		F_1^P	...	F_i^P	...	F_n^P	
		$c_{11}, \ldots, c_{1w_1}$	...	$c_{i1}, \ldots, c_{iw_i}$	...	$c_{n1}, \ldots, c_{nw_n}$	
Project context profile	S^P	s_{P1}	...	s_{Pi}	...	s_{Pn}	
USEPack context profiles	S^{U_1}	s_{11}	...	s_{1i}	...	s_{1n}	
	$\vdots$	$\vdots$		$\vdots$		$\vdots$	
	S^{U_k}	s_{k1}	...	s_{ki}	...	s_{kn}	
	$\vdots$	$\vdots$		$\vdots$		$\vdots$	
	S^{U_v}	s_{v1}	...	s_{vi}	...	s_{vn}	

of context factor characteristics in the i-th context factor. Table 6.2 summarizes the project context factors and the associated USEPacks context profiles.

To calculate the matching of a USEPack U_k for deployment in a project P with respect to the context factor $\tilde{C}_i^P$ the measure $m_{ki} \in [0, 1]$ is introduced. m_{ki} calculates the matching between $\tilde{C}_i^P$ and $\tilde{C}_i^{U_k}$.

For the related problem of measuring the distance between fuzzy sets, a number of metrics are available. A typical example is the generalized relative hamming distance (Kaufmann, 1975).

$$m_{ki} = \frac{1}{w_i} \sum_{l=1}^{w_i} \left| \mu_{\tilde{C}_i^P}(c_{il}) - \mu_{\tilde{C}_i^{U_k}}(c_{il}) \right|$$

These distance metrics calculate the similarity between all elements of two fuzzy sets. But for the problem of selecting appropriate USEPacks for a given project P, characterized by its context profile S^P they do not compute m_{ki} in the intended way. This is illustrated by the following example.

Let $\tilde{C}_i^P$ be a context factor of a project context profile S^P that characterizes a project P.

$$\tilde{C}_i^P = \{(c_{i1}, 0.0), (c_{i2}, 1.0), (c_{i3}, 1.0)\}$$

Let $\tilde{C}_i^{U_1}$ be a context factor of a USEPack context profile S^{U_1} which indicates the characteristics which contributed to the acceptance or rejection of U_1 in past projects.

$$\tilde{C}_i^{U_1} = \{(c_{i1}, 0.0), (c_{i2}, 0.7), (c_{i3}, 0.7)\}$$

Let $\tilde{C}_i^{U_2}$ be a context factor of a USEPack context profile S^{U_2} which indicates the characteristics which contributed to the acceptance or rejection of U_2 in past projects.

$$\tilde{C}_i^{U_2} = \{(c_{i1}, 1.0), (c_{i2}, 1.0), (c_{i3}, 1.0)\}$$

The intuitive interpretation of this constellation is that, with respect to the characteristics F_i^P, U_2 is better suited for deployment in P than U_1 since $\tilde{C}_i^{U_2}$ shows a maximum level of acceptance for all three context characteristics. But if the level of appropriateness of both USEPacks is computed by using the relative hamming distance, the following results are obtained: $m_{1i} = 0.2, m_{2i} = 0.3$. This would mean that USEPack U_1 is more appropriate than USEPack U_2 since the distance between $\tilde{C}_i^P$ and $\tilde{C}_i^{U_1}$ is smaller than the distance between $\tilde{C}_i^P$ and $\tilde{C}_i^{U_2}$. However, this contradicts the intuitive interpretation given above.

In the following an alternative for computing the matching of a USEPack with the context profile S^{U_k} when it is examined under the characteristics F_i^P is presented. The desired matching semantic requires that each USEPack context characteristic value $\mu_{\tilde{C}_i^{U_k}}(c_{ij})$ should be equal to or greater than the respective project context characteristic value $\mu_{C_i^P}(c_{ij})$. The matching measure m_{ki} should only consider the relevant context factor characteristics, i.e. $\{c_{ij}|\mu_{\tilde{C}_i^P}(c_{ij}) = 1\}$. The context factor characteristics that do not apply to the project P, i.e. $\{c_{ij}|\mu_{\tilde{C}_i^P}(c_{ij}) = 0\}$, should be disregarded. Thus the desired matching measure m_{ki} for calculating the matching between $\tilde{C}_i^P$ and $\tilde{C}_i^{U_k}$ should maximize the term:

$$m_{ki} = \frac{1}{w_i} \sum_{j=1}^{w_i} \mu_{\tilde{C}_i^{U_k}}(c_{ij}) \mu_{\tilde{C}_i^P}(c_{ij})$$

This measure is a version of the vector product. It is designed to measure to which degree the relevant context characteristics of $\tilde{C}_i^{U_k}$ match with the context characteristics defined in project context factor $\tilde{C}_i^P$ of project P.

The overall matching $M \in [0, 1]$ of a USEPack U_k for a project P is computed as the mean of all individual context factor matchings m_{ki} between the USEPack context profiles S^{U_k} and a project context profiles S^P. A value of $M(S^P, S^{U_k}) \rightarrow 1$ indicates a high level of support for deploying the USEPack U_k in the project P. Analogously a value of $M(S^P, S^{U_k}) \rightarrow 0$ indicates a low level of support for deploying the USEPack U_k in the project P.

$$M(S^P, S^{U_k}) = \frac{1}{n} \sum_{i=1}^{n} m_{ki}$$

The rationale behind the selection for this approach for aggregating the individual context factor matching values m_{ki} is the additive utility assumption (Triantaphyllou, 2000). This assumption is satisfied as all individual matching values m_{ki} represent benefit. If all criteria represent benefit, then the most preferred alternative is the one for which the sum of all individual matchings is maximized.

For cases in which the additive utility assumption does not apply, different aggregation approaches have been suggested. Examples are the analytical hierarchy process (AHP) and the weighted product model (WPM) (Triantaphyllou, 2000).

6.2 USEPack Assessment Using the Acceptance Model

After each deployment of a USEPack U_k in a Project P the acceptance of the USEPack is assessed by the project team by using the rating scales provided by the acceptance model Q. The acceptance model $Q = \{q_1, \ldots, q_i, \ldots, q_m\}$ consists of a set of acceptance factors q_i. For each acceptance factor n_i items $(h_{i1}, \ldots, h_{ij}, \ldots, h_{in_i})$ and corresponding s-point Likert scales (Judd et al., 1991) to measure the items are provided.

Each item h_{ij} makes a statement about the USEPack U_k concerning the quality factor q_i. Only monotone items are used in these Likert scales, i.e. items that are definitely favorable or unfavorable in their direction. Items that reflect a middle or uncertain position in the issue examined are not used. An example of a monotone item is h_{i1} ="Learning to apply this USEPack is easy for the project team".

Via the rating scales a rating $r_{ij}^{U_k P} \in \lfloor 1, \ldots, s \rfloor$ is assigned to each item. The first point on each s-point rating scale represents a strong disagreement of the project team with the statement of the item h_{ij} and is expressed by a rating $r_{ij}^{U_k P} = 1$. The s-th point represents a strong agreement of the project team with the statement of the item h_{ij} and is expressed by the rating $r_{ij}^{U_k P} = s$. The middle point on the s-point rating scale should reflect a neutral rating of the assessed item. A value for "non-applicable" is not provided on the rating scales, as the items are selected to be applicable to each USEPack. The normalized sum of all ratings for the individual items of an acceptance factor q_i is a measure for the acceptance of the USEPack U_k concerning the acceptance factor q_i. It is scaled to the interval $[-1, 1]$ for later usage in the adaptation of USEPack context profiles described in the next section.

The normalized sum of all scores of all acceptance factors q_i is a measure for the acceptance of the USEPack U_k as perceived by the project team in the project P.

$$R^{U_k P} = \frac{1}{m} \sum_{i=1}^{m} \frac{2}{s \cdot n_i} \sum_{j=1}^{n_i} r_{ij}^{U_k P} - 1$$

$R^{U_k P} \to 1$ indicates a high acceptance of the USEPack U_k by the project team in project P while $R^{U_k P} \to -1$ indicates a low acceptance of the USEPack U_k. by the project team in Project P. Each measurement $R^{U_k P}$ gathered after deploying U_k in a Project P is used to adapt the context profile of the respective USEPack U_k as described in the following section.

6.3 USEPack Context Profiles Adaptation

Based on the acceptance rating $R^{U_k P}$ assigned to the USEPack U_k by the project team in project P, the context profiles S^{U_k} of U_k is adapted.

The goal of the adaptation is that S^{U_k} reflects the project context factor settings under which U_k was accepted or rejected by project teams. For each context factor characteristic this means: if U_k was accepted by project teams in projects P, $\mu_{\tilde{C}_i^{U_k}}(c_{ij})$ is increased, i.e. the distance between $\mu_{\tilde{C}_i^{U_k}}(c_{ij})$ and $\mu_{\tilde{C}_i^P}(c_{ij})$ is decreased. On the other hand, if U_k was rejected by project teams in projects P, $\mu_{\tilde{C}_i^{U_k}}(c_{ij})$ is decreased, i.e. the distance between $\mu_{\tilde{C}_i^{U_k}}(c_{ij})$ and $\mu_{\tilde{C}_i^P}(c_{ij})$ is increased. Only those USEPack context characteristic values $\mu_{\tilde{C}_i^{U_k}}(c_{ij})$ of USEPack U_k are adapted which are relevant in the project context profile S^{U_k} of project P in which the USEPack U_k was deployed, i.e. only those USEPack context characteristic values $\mu_{\tilde{C}_i^{U_k}}(c_{ij})$ are adapted for which the corresponding project context characteristics $\mu_{\tilde{C}_i^P}(c_{ij}) = 1$.

Furthermore, the adaptation should be strong, if extreme high or extreme low acceptance ratings $R^{U_k P}$ were assigned to U_k. Neutral ratings of the USEPack should not lead to an adaptation of S^{U_k}. This can be achieved by updating the USEPack context characteristic value $\mu_{\tilde{C}_i^{U_k}}(c_{ij})$ with the weighted distance between $\mu_{\tilde{C}_i^{U_k}}(c_{ij})$ and $\mu_{\tilde{C}_i^P}(c_{ij})$.

These requirements are satisfied by adapting the USEPack context characteristic value $\mu_{\tilde{C}_i^{U_k}}(c_{ij})$ of the USEPack context factor $\tilde{C}_i^{U_k}$ according to the following equations:

$$\text{if } g \geq 0 : \mu_{\tilde{C}_i^{U_k}}(c_{ij})^* = \mu_{\tilde{C}_i^{U_k}}(c_{ij}) + g \cdot \mu_{\tilde{C}_i^P}(c_{ij}) \left(1 - \mu_{\tilde{C}_i^{U_k}}(c_{ij})\right)$$

$$\text{i } g < 0 f : \mu_{\tilde{C}_i^{U_k}}(c_{ij})^* = \mu_{\tilde{C}_i^{U_k}}(c_{ij}) + g \cdot \mu_{\tilde{C}_i^P}(c_{ij}) \left(\mu_{\tilde{C}_i^{U_k}}(c_{ij})\right)$$

The adaptation factor g is defined by the following equation:

$$g = \frac{1}{c}(R^{U_k P})^3 \in \left[-\frac{1}{c}, \frac{1}{c}\right], c > 1$$

The parameter c is used to control the strength of the adaptation. The parameter c should be selected in a way that considerable changes of context factor characteristic values require a number of consistent positive or negative assessments. This prevents context factor characteristic values to indicate a strong acceptance or rejection after a single positive or negative assessment. The run of g for $c = 10$ is depicted in Fig. 6.1.

The selection of the function for computing the adaptation factor g influences the dynamic behavior of a context profile. For example, a sigmoid function which is steep in the zero-crossing is less suitable as it would lead to an unstable context profile if most ratings are close to a neutral assessment.

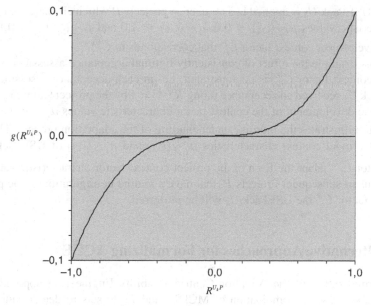

Fig. 6.1 Graph of the g-function

The following example illustrates the effect of consistent positive assessments on the adaptation of a USEPack context factor $\tilde{C}_i^{U_k}$ of a USEPack U_k (Fig. 6.2)

The context factor $\tilde{C}_i^{U_k}$ has the three context characteristics c_{i1}, c_{i2} and c_{i3}. The initial context characteristic values $\mu_{\tilde{C}_i^{U_k}}(c_{i1}) = 0.5$, $\mu_{\tilde{C}_i^{U_k}}(c_{i2}) = 0.5$ and $\mu_{\tilde{C}_i^{U_k}}(c_{i3}) = 0.5$ suggest that little is known about the acceptance or rejection of the USEPack U_k regarding the context factor characteristics.

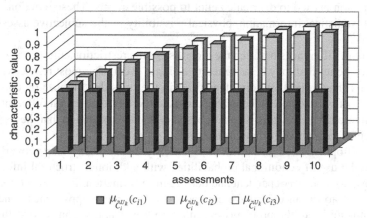

Fig. 6.2 Adaptation of the characteristic values of context factor $\tilde{C}_i^{U_k}$

The USEPack U_k is applied in a number of projects P which all share the context characteristic values $\mu_{\tilde{C}_i^P}(c_{i1}) = 0.0$, $\mu_{\tilde{C}_i^P}(c_{i2}) = 1.0$ and $\mu_{\tilde{C}_i^P}(c_{i3}) = 1.0$ for the respective project context factor $\tilde{C}_i^P$ that corresponds to $\tilde{C}_i^{U_k}$.

In this example the effect of consistently optimal acceptance assessments of U_k on the context factor $\tilde{C}_i^{U_k}$ is demonstrated, i.e. in each acceptance assessment the USEPack U_k received an acceptance rating $R^{U_k P} = 1$ by the project team. Figure 6.2 shows the development of the context factor characteristic values $\mu_{\tilde{C}_i^{U_k}}(c_{ij})$ of $\tilde{C}_i^{U_k}$. The figure illustrates the intuitive understanding of the adaptation process. The two relevant project context characteristics $\mu_{\tilde{C}_i^{U_k}}(c_{i2})$ and $\mu_{\tilde{C}_i^{U_k}}(c_{i3})$ of USEPack context factor $\tilde{C}_i^{U_k}$ adapt the form of the project context factor characteristic values of $\tilde{C}_i^P$. Thus in subsequent Projects P' that have a similar configuration of the project context factor $\tilde{C}_i^P$ the USEPack U_k will be preferred.

6.4 Alternative Approaches for Formalizing ACUE

The formalization of the Adoption-Centric Usability Engineering approach presented above uses a combination of MCDM and fuzzy sets to detect patterns of USEPack method acceptance and rejection. USEPacks are selected for deployment in a project if they have been accepted in previous projects with a similar context. The decision for the selection of USEPacks for future projects is based on accumulated data that indicates that they have been accepted in similar projects in the past.

Many other approaches exist for coping with uncertainty in decision-making situations. They are based on the main formal theories to handle uncertainty: probability theory (Lindley, 1975), possibility theory and evidence theory (Dempster, 1967); (Shafer, 1976).

The basic problem which all theories aim to solve is to estimate the degree to which several uncertain events are believed to occur. Each theory provides formalisms to identify the most believed event. In all theories some kind of assignment function is used to distribute belief to possible events. These functions can be based on statistical information, physical possibility or the subjective assessments of experts.

The main differences between the theories are the restrictions they impose on the amount of belief that may be assigned to a single event. The most restrictive one is probability theory. Furthermore, they differ in the rules they impose on combining the effects of two or more belief distributions gathered from several different pieces of information. The way this is done is based on the interpretation that the respective theory gives to the belief it assigns to events.

A more sophisticated formalism of probability theory is Bayesian network. They combine the use of conditional probabilities with additional structural information that allows to model independent and dependent information. It is beyond the scope of this book to do an exhaustive comparison of all these approaches concerning their applicability to the problems examined in this chapter. Considering the comprehensive application of probability, possibility and evidence-theory to complex decision-making problems it can be safely assumed that the problems examined in this chapter could be mapped to these formalisms.

However, several non-formal arguments support the application of a multi-criteria decision-making approach. First of all the MCDM approach is sufficient to solve the problems formulated in the conceptual development of the ACUE approach. Furthermore, many case studies support that the user threshold for the MCDM method is low as MCDM corresponds with the user's intuitive perception of the problem. MCDM based approaches are easy to apply and maintain by project teams which cannot be expected to be familiar with more complex decision-making formalisms. The approach of this work is to select a formalism that is as simple as possible considering the lack of empirical knowledge about dependencies between the modeled context factors. Probably it is reasonable to switch to more sophisticated concepts for handling uncertainty within the ACUE framework as soon as the analysis of data suggests it.

Part III
Operationalization and Validation

Chapter 7
How Effective Is ACUE? An Empirical Case Study

In addition to being a usability engineering methodology, Adoption-Centric Usability Engineering (ACUE) is supplemented by an empirical framework for assessing its effectiveness and improving its usability methods. This chapter presents an approach for evaluating ACUE as well as the results of an empirical study using this approach. The goal of this evaluation was to get initial feedback about whether the concepts of ACUE address the integration problems. Project team members from five software development organizations participated in the evaluation. The results reported in the two evaluation studies reinforce the motivation for the approach and indicate the potential of the ACUE framework and its support infrastructure.

The results confirm several hypotheses on which the proposed approach is based. They show that usability engineering methods are poorly supported by software development organizations and that knowledge about performing usability engineering methods is not readily available. Yet the results indicate that developers strongly regard usability engineering as a reasonable supplement to the software development process. Furthermore, the interviewed software developers would commit themselves to deploying usability engineering methods during development if appropriate methodological support was available. Despite its exploratory nature, the study presented in this chapter supports the assumptions described earlier in this book regarding the lack of integration of usability engineering methods in software development processes.

7.1 Overview of the Study

For the deployment and further development of ProUSE, perceived usefulness and ease-of-use of the approach are not the only important factors. A central issue is whether the method kit – a key element of the approach – matches with the processes practiced by the project teams.

To ensure successful adoption of a usability engineer (UE) method, the support tool must be highly compatible with the current processes in a project's development lifecycle. This compatibility is particularly relevant for the ACUE approach. Compatibility needs to be addressed at the levels of the approach, structure and design of the support tool.

A. Seffah, E. Metzker, *Adoption-centric Usability Engineering*,
DOI 10.1007/978-1-84800-019-3_7, © Springer-Verlag London Limited 2009

Thus the evaluation was performed in two steps. The first step addressed the compatibility issue. Interviews were performed with process experts to examine whether UE method kits are compatible with the processes practiced in the respective development organizations. This was achieved by eliciting descriptions of practiced processes and by comparing these descriptions with a sample UE method kit. The second step addressed whether the ACUE approach as it is embodied in the ProUSE support system is well accepted by project teams. To answer this question, it was first necessary to examine how the integration problem described in Chapter 2 is perceived by software engineering teams. Next, data was collected to estimate the usefulness of the approach for software engineering teams. As a by-product, we received initial feedback for improving the ProUSE support tool.

Davis' technology acceptance model (TAM) (Davis, 1986) was used as a framework for the study. To achieve the objectives of the second evaluation step, TAM's assessment dimensions of perceived usefulness and perceived ease-of-use were extended by the dimension of understandability. Understandability was examined with a knowledge test; perceived usefulness was studied with qualitative effects analysis (Kitchenham, 1996); and perceived ease-of-use was examined by studying user behavior during the use of the support system.

The context of the two evaluations as well as details on objectives, subjects, methods, tasks, and procedure are described in the following sections.

7.1.1 Goals of the Study

The primary goals of this exploratory study were:

1. To examine the development processes as they are perceived by the process experts of the respective organizations
2. To identify which interfaces can be identified between the practiced development processes and the UE method kit
3. To examine where the practiced processes and the UE method kit differ

7.1.2 Materials: The UE Method Kit

The UE method kit forms the basis for integrating UE techniques into the software engineering process. Figure 7.1 illustrates an instantiation of the UE method kit by the DaimlerChrysler research group (Metzker and Offergeld, 2001). The bold text in the top row represents the process phases of the method kit. The items below each process phase are the corresponding usability engineering process goals. For example, the usability engineering process goal "define user profiles" is achieved in the requirements analysis process phase.

Project preparation	Requirements analysis	User interface design	Evaluation and testing	Introduction and operation
Cost/benefit analysis	Business goals	Workflow reengineering	Usability tests	System approval
Integr. usability in contract	User profiles	Conceptual UI Model	Design optimization	User manual
Def. of usability roles	User tasks	User interface mockups	Support of implement.	User training
Planning of process	Physical environment	Iterative UI walkthroughs		Elicit enduser feedback
User involvement plan	HW/SW constraints	Software UI prototypes		Plan release change
Usability trainings	Design guidelines	Iterative usability tests		
	Usability goals	UI styleguides		
		Detailed design		

Fig. 7.1 Method kit based on the DaimlerChryser UE methodology

7.1.3 Subjects

A total of ten process experts (eight men, two women) from five different organizations participated in the survey. Ages varied between 26 and 44 years with an average of 8.5 years of relevant professional experience. The most frequently cited project duties were requirements analysis, user interface design and project concept development. More than half of the subjects (n=6) stated that they were also involved in project management, development, and usability evaluation and systems tests.

The subjects were involved in a number of different projects where usability was expected to play a major role (n=8). Almost half of the projects in which the subjects participated were additionally developing Web-based systems (n=4). Two projects were also developing embedded systems. Agent-based systems, augmented reality systems and gesture recognition systems were mentioned as typical systems developed by the project groups. The average development duration for a product was 19.1 months.

7.1.4 Method

At the beginning of the interviews, we elicited information on professional experience, current position, type of products developed and the common approach applied in developing software systems. The core of the survey consists of a semi-structured interview in which the subjects described their development process.

The interviews were opened with a common question regarding the processes currently practiced in the development team. To ensure an uninfluenced description of the development process, no notional or structural guidelines were given to the subjects. Instead, the subjects were asked to sketch their understanding of the central process elements of their development process and to describe these elements and their interrelationships. The purpose of this approach was to make it easy for the subjects to provide a first rough structuring of their descriptions.

Afterward, each subject was asked to add details to their description by describing the activities which they associated with each process element. In addition, they were asked which roles participated in each activity and which utilities were used to support the activities. The descriptions of the subjects were recorded in writing. These descriptions provided an overview of the processes practiced in the organizations and allowed for a comparison with the UE method kit.

At the end of each interview, the subjects were asked to identify the activities in the UE method kit that were also practiced in their processes. The identification was performed using a depiction of the UE method kit as shown in Fig. 7.1. Additionally, subjects could name activities that were not included in the UE method kit.

Each interview took about 1.5–2 hours and was performed by one interviewer. The interviews were recorded by a second person in a pre-structured table.

7.2 Results

The following sections present the results of the process sketching sessions and the comparison of practiced processes with processes in the sample UE method kit. Due to the exploratory nature of this study, in many cases there are only a few instances of a given class of subject behavior. However the goal of this study is not to arrive at quantitative results, but rather to identify problems for further study and to improve the ProUSE concepts.

7.3 Process Sketches

Only half of the project groups examined in this study used a standard as a basis for the system development process. In three cases, ISO usability standards were used. One project group used an adapted version of the waterfall model (also called V-Model) together with explicit programming guidelines.

The development processes sketched by the subjects consisted of six process phases on average, varying between four and ten phases. In two teams, there was a strong compatibility between the described processes and the sample UE method kit depicted in Fig. 7.1. These processes differed only in the omission of single process phases. One subject did not describe an explicit planning phase, and another subject omitted the phases "deployment" and "maintenance".

Many subjects described a more differentiated division of the process into phases. For example, one subject described four phases that could be assigned to the requirements analysis phase of the UE method kit. Compared to the UE method kit (6 phases), subjects tended to describe more phases (minimum: 4; maximum: 10; average: 7).

The order of phases varied between project groups. For example, one subject stated that the requirements analysis phase is followed by the "revision of project goals" phase – the reverse order from the UE method kit, where revision of projects goals is associated with the earlier phase of project planning.

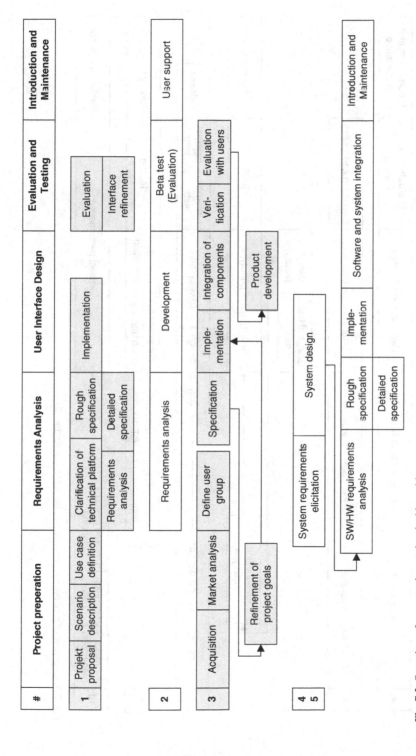

Fig. 7.2 Overview of process phases sketched by subjects

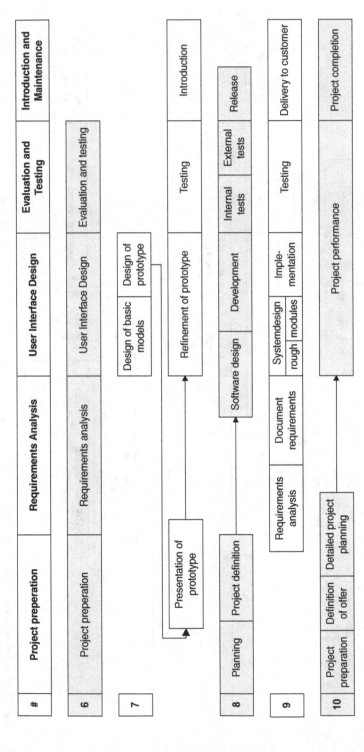

#	Project preperation	Requirements Analysis	User Interface Design	Evaluation and Testing	Introduction and Maintenance
6	Project preperation	Requirements analysis	User Interface Design	Evaluation and testing	
7	Planning / Project definition / Presentation of prototype		Design of basic models / Design of prototype	Refinement of prototype / Testing	Introduction
8	Planning / Project definition	Software design	Development	Internal tests / External tests / Release	
9	Requirements analysis	Document requirements	Systemdesign / rough / modules / Imple-mentation	Testing	Delivery to customer
10	Project preparation / Definition of offer / Detailed project planning	Project performance			Project completion

Fig. 7.3 Overview of process phases sketched by subjects (continued)

Phase 1	Phase 2	Phase 3	Phase 3	Phase 4	Phase 5	Phase 6	Phase 7	Phase 8	Activities
System requirements analysis	System design	Software/ hardware requirements	Rough specification of components	Detailed specification of components	Implementation	Software integration	System Integration	Deployment	
Define requirements	Technical design	Specification of hardware requirements	Create software architecture	Create software architecture	Implementation of objects	Integration of objects	Integration of components	Integration of components	
	Define external Interface	Specification of software requirements	Define internal interfaces	Develop internal interfaces	Module testing	Documentation/proof of testing	Documentation/ Proof of funct. of SW units	Internal acceptance	
					Documentation		Documentation/ Proof of funct. of HW units	External acceptance	

Fig. 7.4 Example of a method kit sketch with many phases and few steps

Subjects explicitly described the iterative nature of the design and testing phases. This iterative nature is not captured by the UE method kit in its current form.

Figures 7.2 and 7.3 show an overview of the process phases sketched by subjects. At the top of both figures, the process phases of the UE method kit introduced in Fig. 7.1 are depicted. The subjects' process phase sketches are aligned according to the phases of the UE method kit to allow for a better comparison. The number to the left of each sketch refers to the number of the subject who provided the information.

Six of the subjects named phases associated with the project planning phase and eight named phases that were associated with the requirements analysis phase. All ten subjects named phases that correspond to the phases of design, development, and testing. Six subjects identified the deployment phase and three subjects identified the maintenance phase.

The number of process activities varied considerably between subjects. Some subjects named many process activities for each phase. For example, subject #10 assigned five to thirteen process activities to each phase. However, this subject named a relatively small number of phases (see Fig. 7.3).

Other subjects named few process activities for each phase. For example, Subject #5 named just three process steps per phase while their whole process consisted of eight phases. An example of such a process sketch is depicted in Fig. 7.4.

Compared to the method kit that contains 30 process steps, the subjects named fewer process steps (mean 20; range 7–28).

7.4 Matching of the Method Kit with Practiced Development Processes

The results of the direct comparison with the UE method kit are depicted in Fig. 7.5. The number below each phase or activity indicates the number of subjects who stated that the phase or activity was also practiced in their development process. All phases of the method kit were identified by the majority of the subjects as a part of their development process. The project preparation, requirements analysis and test phases were identified by all subjects.

Classical project activities such as Offer and contract, Planning and role assignment, Identification of hardware and software constraints, User training and System extensions were identified by most subjects as part of their practiced development process. Activities that are more specific to usability engineering, such as User profile analysis, Definition of usability goals, User interface mockups, User interface walkthroughs and Iterative usability tests were identified by relatively few subjects.

The processes as described by the subjects show many commonalities but also remarkable differences between each other and in comparison to the UE method kit.

The phases of the UE method kit can be identified in most process sketches. The phases of "project preparation" and "deployment and maintenance" are the most often omitted phases. However, cueing subjects with the UE method kit at the end

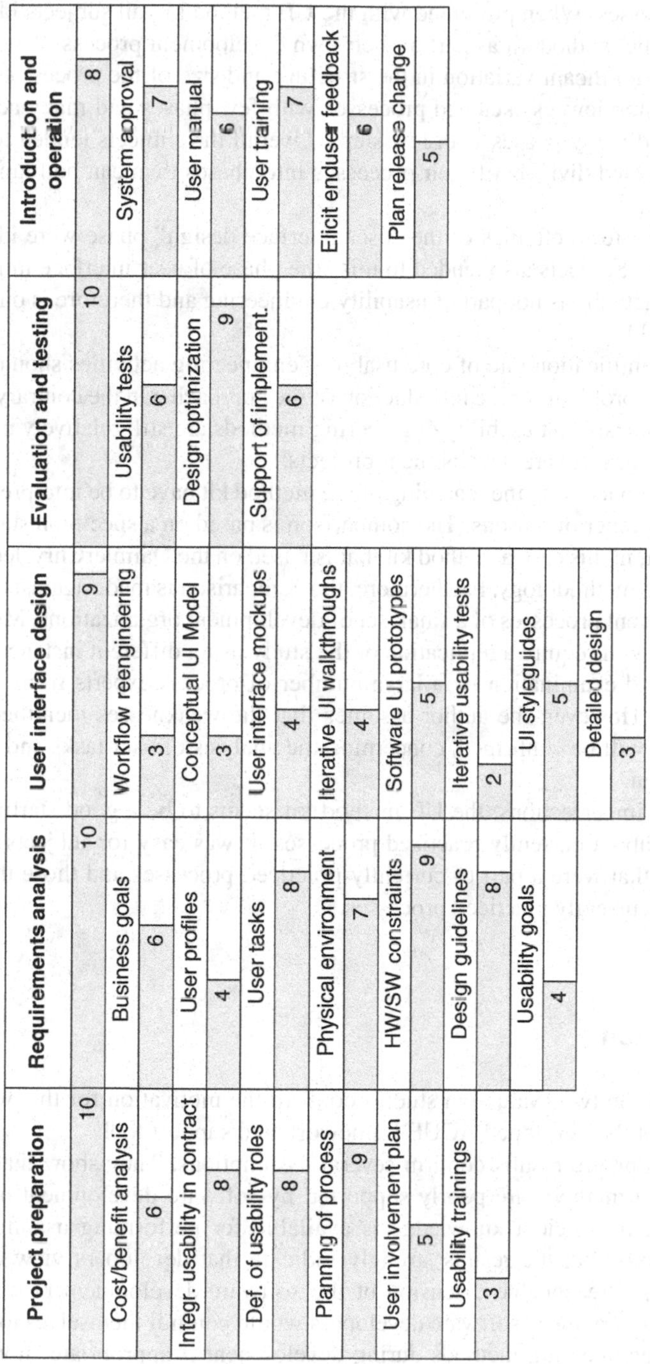

Project preparation	Requirements analysis	User interface design	Evaluation and testing	Introduction and operation
10	10	9	10	8
Cost/benefit analysis	Business goals	Workflow reengineering	Usability tests	System approval
6	6	3	6	7
Integr. usability in contract	User profiles	Conceptual UI Model	Design optimization	User manual
8	4	3	9	6
Def. of usability roles	User tasks	User interface mockups	Support of implement.	User training
8	8	4	6	7
Planning of process	Physical environment	Iterative UI walkthroughs		Elicit enduser feedback
9	7	4		6
User involvement plan	HW/SW constraints	Software UI prototypes		Plan release change
5	9	5		5
Usability trainings	Design guidelines	Iterative usability tests		
3	8	2		
	Usability goals	UI styleguides		
	4	5		
		Detailed design		
		3		

Fig. 7.5 Identification of practiced activities

of the interview shows that these omissions are caused by an incomplete recall of the practiced processes. When presented with the UE method kit, all subjects identified the phases of the method kit as part of their own development process.

There was significant variation in the structure and size of the process sketches. While some interviewees sketched processes with few phases and many activities, others sketched many phases with few steps. Overall the subjects tended toward a more differentiated division of their processes into phases than can be found in the UE method kit.

Furthermore, few activities of the "user interface design" phase were identified by the subjects. Subjects also tended to miss the phase of user interface implementation, which actually is not part of usability engineering and therefore is omitted in the UE method kit.

The low identification rate of core usability engineering activities should not be interpreted as a problem for the introduction of the approach. On the contrary, it confirms the hypothesis that usability engineering methods are still relatively unknown and underused in software development projects.

The results concerning the matching of the method kit have to be interpreted cautiously for a number of reasons. The comparison is based on a specific instance of a UE method kit, in this case a method kit that is based on the DaimlerChrysler usability engineering methodology. Furthermore, the comparison is made against the practiced development processes of a small set of development organizations. More conclusive results will require a replication of the study using different instances of UE method kits and examination by a large number of process experts from different organizations. However, the author assumes that the weaknesses identified in the core practices will be confirmed, concerning the analysis of user tasks and the user interface design.

Despite its imperfections, the UE method kit seems to be a good starting point for reflecting about currently practiced processes. It was easy for subjects to identify activities that were a part of currently practiced processes and those that were missing from currently practiced processes.

7.5 Discussion

The results of the two evaluation studies confirm the motivation for this work and the potential of the developed ACUE framework and support tool.

The questionnaire results confirm several assumptions. They show that usability engineering methods are poorly supported by software development organizations and that insufficient knowledge is available for performing usability engineering methods. Yet the results strongly indicate that developers view usability engineering as a reasonable extension of the software development process. Furthermore, the interviewed software developers would commit themselves to deploying usability engineering methods during development if appropriate support was available.

Another basic assumption confirmed by the results is that there is no strong separation of development tasks within the development teams. User interface development accounts for 26–39% of all development activities. This underscores that it is not sufficient to install a usability engineer in a project – rather there is a need to transfer usability engineering knowledge to the whole project team. The results show that the interviewees of the UE group are also developers but are somewhat more focused on user interface development.

As shown in the study, the interviewees drew most of their process knowledge from professional experience. This supports an experience-based approach to the introduction and establishment of usability engineering methods, as proposed in Adoption-Centric Usability Engineering.

The interviews of the process experts show that the examined organizations employ highly diverse development processes. The process sketches differed significantly in the breadth of the processes described and also in the level of detail in which major process phases are structured. However, when the process experts were shown an example of a UE method kit, they encountered no problems in identifying phases and activities that were part of their practiced processes. This indicates that process experts can easily map their mental model of the development process to the UE method kit.

However, cueing subjects with the UE method kit also showed that many essential UE activities are still unknown or underused in typical software development projects. Again, this reinforces the motivation for systematically triggering organizational learning and for introducing the required knowledge to project teams.

The three subject groups – new employees, software engineers, and usability engineers – showed no special demographic properties. It can be assumed that the distribution of age, gender, education, and professional experience is typical for such subject groups.

In particular, the qualitative data indicate that the support system and the basic structure of ProUSE are very positively viewed by the subject groups. These systems were appreciated by subjects for their ability to impart methodological knowledge, and because they support capturing and systematic reuse of practical experiences. This appreciation can be linked to the finding that among project team members, professional experience is the major source of process knowledge.

The behavioral data and the think aloud protocols indicate that the ProUSE support system still has potential for improvement regarding self-descriptiveness and consistency between modules of the system. The terms selected for describing some constructs were not always self-explanatory.

Despite the exploratory nature of this research, the studies presented in this chapter support the hypotheses about the lack of integration of usability engineering methods in software development processes and the need experienced by project teams for support in performing usability engineering methods. The evaluation of the ACUE support tool indicates that the ACUE approach is accepted by software practitioners and is perceived as a solution for improving the effectiveness of UE activities. This is an important precondition for a successful and lasting application of the ACUE approach in software development organizations.

Chapter 8
Putting it into Practice: The ProUse Tool

The description of the Adoption-Centric Usability Engineering (ACUE) approach has not yet been associated with a specific technology. In this chapter, constraints are examined for an appropriate operationalization of the ACUE framework. These constraints influenced the development of a Web-based support environment called ProUSE, which implements the concepts of the ACUE approach. The core functions of the support environment and its architecture are described. The user interacts with the system via a Web-portal and three components that support method kit configuration as well as method guidance, method capturing, and maintenance. The usage of these components is described based on a scenario of the system's intended use.

8.1 Constraints for Operationalizing the ACUE

The ACUE approach does not require the use of a special technology. For example, it would be possible to practice ACUE using only paper and pencil. Printed forms could be provided for Usability Engineering Experience Packages (USEPacks), context models and artifacts. Printed spreadsheets could be developed for assessing USEPacks and adapting context models.

However, a paper-based operationalization of ACUE would largely depend on human accuracy and strong commitment to avoiding inconsistencies and errors. Even for a relatively small pool of USEPacks, the tasks of searching for appropriate USEPacks and keeping existing USEPacks consistent with changing context models would soon become too time-consuming and error-prone without appropriate support.

In general the selection of a technology to operationalize ACUE depends on a number of constraints applying to the target environment in which ACUE is deployed. One of the most important factors is the existence of other tools in the target environment that could be used as a technological base for implementing an ACUE support environment. Typical candidates for such systems are groupware, project management and knowledge management systems already used in the target environment.

A. Seffah, E. Metzker, *Adoption-centric Usability Engineering*,
DOI 10.1007/978-1-84800-019-3_8, © Springer-Verlag London Limited 2009

Building on such existing systems has two main advantages. First, initial invest-
ments in new software platforms are minimized. Second, the training of project
teams in using the support environment is minimized.

However, the prototype support system developed in this research is subject to
additional constraints. In the most comprehensive and visionary scenario of use, the
support system should be accessible by project teams collaborating across different
organizations. Each organization should be able to access the method pool, apply
the UE methods in its respective context and feed back experiences with and assessments of the UE methods used. For this reason the support environment should not
be based on a single groupware or knowledge management system used in one of
the organizations.

Considering this generic and comprehensive scenario of use, it is reasonable to
implement a Web-based support environment which is not tightly integrated with
specific existing groupware tools. This Web-based support environment concen-
trates on the core aspects of the ACUE approach instead of optimizing the inter-
operability with existing systems. The usability of the system is ensured by integrating UE methods such as paper prototyping, cognitive walkthroughs, heuristic
evaluations and usability tests into the development process.

The operationalization of the ACUE framework required the formalization of the
underlying concepts. Nevertheless, the support system should hide the complexity
of the ACUE concepts and computations from the project team. The data required
by the approach should be easy to gather and maintain by development teams. The
project team should not require the help of a separate organization in order to operate
the system.

Understanding the practical value of UE methods and optimizing their deployment in development processes obviously is not a core business of development
teams. Therefore the ACUE support system needs to provide a high level of
perceived utility to the project team and it should be easy to understand, learn,
and use.

8.2 Structure and Main Feature

Based on the constraints described in the previous section, a Web-based tool was
developed to support ACUE. In this section the core functions of the support environment that are visible for project personnel are briefly described and the architecture of the system is explained.

A central goal of the envisioned system is to make UE methods easily accessible
to project teams and to support project teams in deploying UE methods in their
projects. These UE methods are captured as USEPacks.

The project team is supported by the system in collecting data on the acceptance
of the usability engineering methods deployed. This data is exploited to improve
decisions on selecting appropriate usability engineering methods. For this purpose,
the system needs to provide a way to evaluate and integrate project team feedback
on the acceptance and optimal context of use of the deployed methods.

The project team is supported by the system in selecting optimal usability engineering methods based on particular project characteristics and previous assessments of the acceptance of the usability engineering methods. The system supports project teams in maintaining the pool of available usability engineering methods by providing means for creating new USEPacks and evolving existing USEPacks.

Figure 8.1 shows the architecture of the ProUSE system that was developed to implement these functions. The system consists of three layers: the data layer, the services layer, and the presentation layer. The overall system is based on the client server paradigm. All elements of the data layer as well as the service layer reside on the server. The components of the presentation layer reside on the clients.

The data layer provides structures to store the method kits, USEPacks, context models, quality models and artifacts.

The services layer provides lower-level services for data processing and communication between clients and server as well as higher-level services that implement

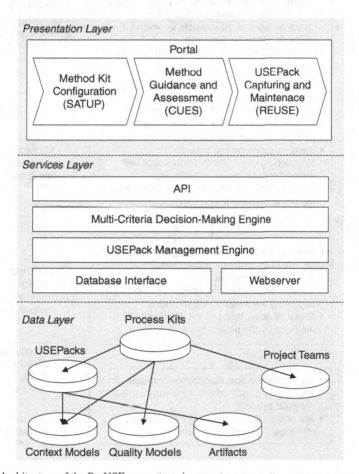

Fig. 8.1 Architecture of the ProUSE support environment

the main logic of the support tool. A Web server component is used to transmit components of the presentation layer and data to the clients and send requests from clients to the server. Furthermore, the service layer provides an interface that abstracts from the data structures of the data layer and provides objects for the main concepts such as method kits, USEPacks and context models. The USEPack management engine provides services for operations on USEPacks such as creating, storing, changing and deleting USEPacks while keeping the method pool in a consistent state.

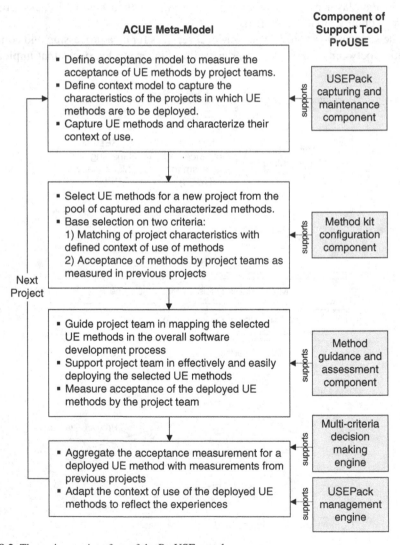

Fig. 8.2 The main user interface of the ProUSE portal

The multi-criteria decision-making engine facilitates the ranking of USEPacks based on defined project characteristics and required quality criteria. It provides mechanisms for comparing USEPacks based on the similarity of their context descriptions. The context models that are used to model characteristics of methods and projects are defined as sets of fuzzy sets. Based on these models, the engine is able to compute similarity measures for projects and methods to facilitate decisions based on analogy.

The decision-making engine is coupled with the assessment component: if a method receives a poor assessment in a given project context, the method's characteristics are automatically adapted to reduce the probability of the method being selected in similar projects. On the other hand, if a method has been applied successfully in a certain project, its characteristics are adapted to increase its probability of selection in similar projects in the future.

An Application Programming Interface (API) encapsulates these services to provide objects and additional services to render USEPacks, context models, method kits and other concepts of ACUE for the applications of the presentation layer.

The applications of the presentation layer provide a user interface that clusters and presents the underlying functionality of the system according to the user's tasks.

Figure 8.2 shows how the elements of the support tool are related to the steps of the ACUE meta-model. The components support the steps of the ACUE meta-model introduced previously.

In the following sections, the functionality of the support environment is described based on its intended use. The descriptions focus on the components of the presentation layer.

8.3 ProUSE Portal

The system can either be installed in the organization's intranet or accessed via the Internet if the project involves collaboration among multiple organizations. The project team can log into the system via the ProUSE portal depicted in Fig. 8.3.

Logging into the system via the ProUSE portal serves a number of purposes. First, it prevents unauthorized users from accessing the data stored in the system. Second, the profiles stored for each authorized user speed up the USEPack creation process, as data such as name and affiliation of a USEPack author can be automatically supplemented by the system. Third, the profiles keep track of the USEPacks and method kits that have been accessed recently by the user, allowing the user to pick up their work where they left off in the previous session.

After logging in, the support environment provides access to the component for method kit configuration (SATUP), method guidance and assessment (CUES) and USEPack capturing and maintenance (REUSE).

These three components adhere to a common user interface design principle: the wizard principle. According to this design approach, a complex task is decomposed

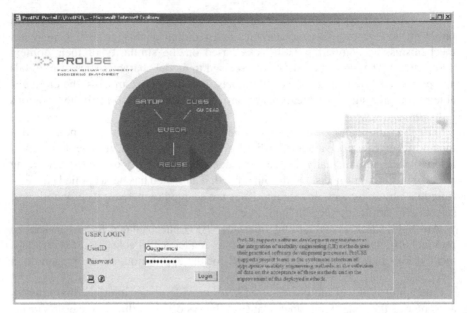

Fig. 8.3 The ProUSE portal

into a linear series of subtasks. Instead of confronting the user with all user interface elements for all subtasks on one screen, the user is guided through the subtasks by the system step-by-step. Only the relevant subset of controls for the current subtask is presented to the user.

Figure 8.4 shows how this principle was deployed for the three components SATUP, CUES and REUSE and how the user navigates in the system. On top of each component, a navigation bar allows switching between the main components: SATUP, CUES and REUSE. The navigation bar also allows the user to display help information and to log out of the system. Beneath the top navigation, the component name is displayed and a tab pane is provided for direct navigation to individual working steps. The section beneath this one shows the name of the object that is currently in use, for example the name of a method kit or a USEPack. In the main working area, the individual working steps are carried out. The layout of this area depends on the specific tasks, but consistent interaction is ensured for handling similar tasks. In the left bottom section of the screen, a short explanation of the current subtask supports first-time or casual users. In the right bottom section of the screen, navigation buttons allow users to move forward and backward between individual working steps.

This general workflow and screen layout is consistently applied to all three components discussed in the following section. We therefore do not describe each individual working step of the workflow but instead focus on the core tasks that are accomplished by each component.

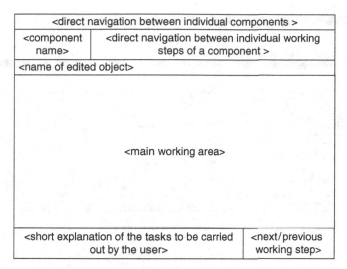

<direct navigation between individual components >	
<component name>	<direct navigation between individual working steps of a component >
<name of edited object>	
<main working area>	
<short explanation of the tasks to be carried out by the user>	<next/ previous working step>

Fig. 8.4 User interface structure of a ProUSE component

8.4 Method Kit Configuration

Once it is decided which usability engineering methods are required for the project, an appropriate method kit is configured by the project team using the method kit configuration component of ProUse. The system presents an unconfigured method kit to the project team. The project team then chooses a name for the method kit and briefly describes the usability aspects of the project in textual form.

In the next step, the project-specific constraints are mapped to the project context profile of the method kit. This is done by adjusting the context factors of the context profile to reflect the characteristics of the project. Examples of context factors are the experience of the development team in the application domain and the spatial distribution of the development team.

Next, the system presents a visual representation of the phases and usability engineering activities of the method kit, in tabular form. The initial phases and corresponding UE activities are predefined. They can be tailored by the project team so that irrelevant UE activities are omitted.

Figure 8.5 shows an example of configuring a method kit. The phases of the method kit are displayed in bold text in the top row of the method kit. In the column beneath each phase, the associated usability engineering activities are displayed.

Once selecting on a usability engineering activity in the method kit, the user triggers a search for USEPacks that can achieve the activity. The results are displayed in the table in the lower half of the main working area beneath the method kit. Each row of the table represents a USEPack candidate that can be deployed to perform the respective usability activity.

The table shows a set of data that can be used by the project team to make a decision about selecting a USEPack for deployment. For each USEPack, a measure

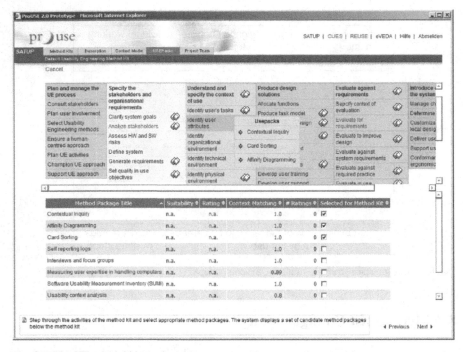

Fig. 8.5 The UE method kit configuration component

is provided for the degree of match between the project context profile of the method kit and the USEPack context profile. This matching factor ranges from zero (worst) to one (best).

Another column provides the aggregated acceptance ratings for each USEPack. Again, the rating factor ranges from zero, which indicates no acceptance of the USEPack in past projects, to one, which indicates total acceptance of the USEPack in past projects. Additionally, the aggregated acceptance rating factor, the context matching factor and the number of total ratings are provided for each USEPack. The project team can examine each candidate USEPack in a read-only view by clicking on the title of the USEPack in the table.

Based on these data, the project team can use various strategies for selecting appropriate USEPacks. Typically, the project team will select the candidate USEPack that shows the highest matching and rating factors together with the largest number of ratings. If a USEPack is selected, it is associated with the respective usability engineering activity of the method kit.

By stepping through all the usability engineering activities of the method kit, each usability engineering activity is associated with one or more USEPacks. Each usability engineering activity of the method kit for which one or more USEPacks are selected is marked with a USEPack symbol, which resembles a package.

In the last step, the project team members who should have access to the configured method kit are defined. After the configuration of the method kit is completed, the method kit is saved.

8.5 Method Guidance

In the previous step, the SATUP component was used to configure a new usability engineering method kit to match the needs of a specific software development project. Based on this configuration, the system generates a project-specific hypermedia usability engineering workspace. This workspace is accessed by the project team via the CUES component. In CUES, the project team can select a preconfigured method kit to deploy in a project. After a method kit is selected, it is displayed as shown in Fig. 8.6. The project team members can now easily navigate the method kit to access appropriate USEPacks. Since only selected phases, activities and methods are displayed, the project team is shielded from potentially irrelevant methods.

The first step in this navigation is to identify the appropriate starting phase of the method kit based on the current development phase of the project. In the next step, the project team member evaluates whether the usability engineering activities for this phase have already been accomplished. If they have not been accomplished, the

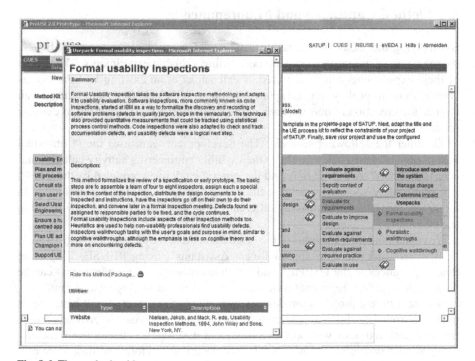

Fig. 8.6 The method guidance component

project team member navigates to this usability engineering activity and the system presents the preconfigured USEPacks that can be deployed to perform this activity.

The USEPack provides the project team members with a detailed description of a usability engineering method and utilities such as examples and reusable templates that facilitate ad hoc deployment of the method. The guidance remains passive and does not enforce the performance of the proposed methods.

After the completion of the project or major project phases, the project team meets to review the method kit and the USEPacks that have been applied. Based on the acceptance model, CUES creates a USEPack assessment form for each USEPack. This form provides a consistent way for the project team to assess the quality of the USEPack.

After the evaluations are submitted by the project team, the system recalculates the context and acceptance profiles of the deployed USEPacks. If a given method was not useful to the development team, the team members assign a poor acceptance rating to the respective USEPack. This will reduce the likelihood of the USEPack being selected in subsequent method kits with the same project context profile. Alternatively, team members can assign high ratings to USEPacks that had a positive impact on their work, thus increasing the likelihood that the respective USEPack will be reused in subsequent projects.

8.6 Method Capturing and Maintenance

By applying the methods and best practices which are described in a USEPack, the members of the project team are performing valuable experiments. The results of these experiments can be captured as extensions of an existing USEPack or as comments on it, or they can be captured in a new USEPack. Such experiments can include the invention of new methods or the adaptation and streamlining of existing methods.

Consider the following scenario: The development team uses the "Contextual Task Analysis" USEPack to perform the usability engineering activity called "Analyze User Tasks". Although they find the general guidelines provided by the USEPack useful, they soon discover that the contextual task analysis for designing an intelligent avatar is fundamentally different from the general method they found in the USEPack.

To capture the modifications of the original method, they create a new USEPack, "Contextual Task Analysis for Intelligent Assistants", using REUSE. They enter their experiences in the USEPack and attach documents and templates that can be reused when performing a contextual task analysis for an intelligent assistant.

The next time a project team designs an intelligent assistant, it will have access to the improved contextual task analysis method and the reusable artifacts. These improvement activities will prevent subsequent development teams from encountering similar problems and will enable those teams to perform the task more efficiently.

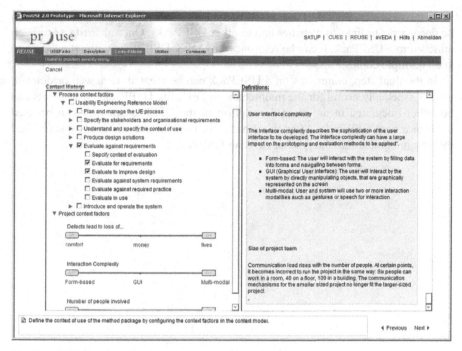

Fig. 8.7 USEPack capturing and maintenance component

Figure 8.7 shows the REUSE component during the creation of a USEPack. The textual description of the USEPack was already entered in the previous subtask. In this step, team members define the initial USEPack context profile for the new USEPack.

By default, the context factors of a USEPack are initialized to reflect that it is not known which context factors contribute to the acceptance or rejection of the USEPack. These default values are changed when a project team applies a USEPack in a project and rates its acceptance. If initial knowledge about the influence of context factors on the rejection or acceptance of the USEPack is available, the initial USEPack context profile can be refined. This refinement of the initial USEPack context profile is depicted in Fig. 8.7.

The hierarchical structure depicted on the left side of the main working area is used to refine the initial USEPack context profile. The structure contains the USEPack context factors and the associated characteristics. The values of the characteristics can be adjusted by the user.

The name of each context factor is linked to background information on the context factor. By clicking on a context factor name, the background information is displayed on the right side of the main working area. This information clarifies the meaning of a context factor and its characteristics and supports the creator of a USEPack in correctly refining the initial context profile.

In the next step, the USEPack is supplemented with artifacts. These artifacts can be documents or links to websites and to other USEPacks. Once an artifact has been attached to a USEPack, it can be referenced by other USEPacks without needing to keep multiple copies.

In the final step, comments on a USEPack can be created, reviewed or deleted. This is especially useful for the maintenance of existing USEPacks. Comments can be either integrated in the main description of the USEPack or they can be used to form a new USEPack. After this final step, the USEPack is usually saved and thereby integrated into the pool of existing USEPacks.

Chapter 9
How Well do ACUE and ProUse Work? Overall Evaluation

To examine whether the ACUE approach as embodied in ProUSE works effectively, an overall evaluation was designed to answer the following questions: Do the project personnel understand the basic principles and structures of the approach without extensive training? How do project teams assess the potential quantitative effects of the approach on their practices? Would they use the approach in their setting? What problems do project teams have in working with the ProUSE support tool for ACUE?

9.1 Evaluation of ProUSE

The goal of the ACUE approach is to improve the integration of UE methods in existing software development processes by measuring their acceptance by project teams. Thus ACUE can also be understood as a process improvement approach.

A large number of process improvement programs end up being cancelled or – in the worst case – fail, because the improvement approach is not accepted at the project team level (Goldenson et al., 1999); (Hughes, 1996), (Laitenberger and Dreyer, 1998); (Niessink and Van Vliet, 1999); (Silverman, 1985). The improvement program can be perceived as tedious and time-consuming by the project team, or the benefit of new methods for daily practice can be perceived as being too low to justify sustained effort.

9.1.1 Context of the Evaluation

The approach was evaluated with the participation of the same five software engineering companies that took part in the study of the method kits described in the previous section, but using different subjects in those companies. The companies were medium to large organizations. The organizations understood the need to improve the usability of their products, but experience with usability engineering was not readily available in the engineering teams.

ProUSE was preconfigured for this study: appropriate context and acceptance models were defined and usability engineering methods were captured in

A. Seffah, E. Metzker, *Adoption-centric Usability Engineering*,
DOI 10.1007/978-1-84800-019-3_9, © Springer-Verlag London Limited 2009

USEPacks. Resources included successful methods invented in previous industrial engineering projects such as reported in Metzker and Offergeld (2001), methods distilled from the literature on usability engineering (Constantine and Lockwood, 1999); (Mayhew, 1999); (Nielsen, 1994), and recent research results such as Spencer's "streamlined cognitive walkthrough" (Spencer, 2000).

9.1.2 Subjects

All 44 subjects participated in the study on a voluntary basis. Of these, 39 were full-time employees working as software engineers for the companies described in Section 3.1. Five subjects were graduate students working for the companies on a part-time basis. The subjects were involved in developing highly interactive software systems in a variety of domains, e.g. driver assistance systems, home entertainment, and military defense systems.

Based on their experience with the development of highly interactive systems, the subjects were classified into three groups: new employees (NE), software engineers (SE), and usability engineers (UE) (Nielsen, 1994). The size of the groups is set out in Table 9.1.

In the following, these groups are referred to as user groups for reasons of simplicity.

9.1.3 Method

The two main research methods were qualitative effects analysis (Kitchenham, 1996) and acceptance studies based on the technology acceptance model (TAM) (Davis, 1986).

In this study, TAM was used as a framework for the evaluation. Motivated by the objectives defined in the introduction of this chapter, TAM's dimension of perceived usefulness was further refined into the following subdimensions:

- Compatibility with daily practice
- Usefulness as a tool
- Support of working tasks
- Increase in knowledge
- Increased efficiency of UE

In addition, TAM's assessment dimensions of perceived usefulness and perceived ease-of-use were extended by the dimension of understandability. This dimension

Table 9.1 Size of subject groups

	New employees	Software engineers	Usability engineers	Total
# of individuals per group	10	21	13	44

examines whether it is easy for the subjects to understand the concepts of the ACUE approach such as context profiles and method kits.

Qualitative effects analysis (Kitchenham, 1996) uses expert opinion to estimate quantitative effects of methods and/or tools on processes and/or products. Thus qualitative effects analysis provides a subjective assessment of the quantitative effect of methods and tools and/or the combined impact of several methods and tools. Sometimes the term "feature analysis" is used to describe a qualitative evaluation.

Qualitative effects analysis belongs to a family of qualitative evaluation methods that can be performed as an experiment, case study or survey. In a qualitative experiment, the evaluation activities are organized more formally by providing a controlled setting and a specific selection of potential experimental subjects. In a qualitative case study, a feature-based evaluation is performed after a method has been used in practice on a real project.

In this study, qualitative effects analysis was performed as a survey after the subjects applied the ACUE support tool to achieve a set of tasks. The tasks were embedded in a scenario that covered the steps of the ACUE meta-model introduced in Section 3.3, such as the configuration of method kits and the creation and assessment of USEPacks.

9.1.4 Data Collection Techniques

The subdimensions of perceived usefulness specified above were measured by qualitative effects analysis while ease-of-use was examined by studying user behavior during the user's interaction with the support environment (Nielsen, 1994). Understandability was examined via a knowledge test in which the subjects answered questions on the concepts of the overall approach and the support environment. The knowledge test was performed before and after the interaction with the tool to study if and how the subjects' understanding of the concepts changed.

For data collection, two basic techniques were deployed: questionnaires and scenario-based tasks. A pre-test questionnaire (Q1) was used to elicit personal data and professional experience of the subjects as well as their understanding of the central concepts of the ACUE approach. A post-test questionnaire (Q2) was used to examine the subjects' understanding of the central concepts of the Adoption-Centric Usability Engineering approach after using the support system and to measure the perceived ease-of-use and usefulness of the system. Details on the purpose of the two questionnaires deployed (Q1 and Q2) are summarized in Table 9.2.

Scenario-based tasks constituted the core of the evaluation. Tasks were specific to user groups. While the subjects were working on a task, behavioral data and any comments made while thinking out loud were captured as a basis for improving the ACUE support environment. Section 9.1.5 describes the tasks that are performed by the subjects while the exact evaluation procedure and deployment of the methods is described in Section 9.1.6.

Table 9.2 Data collected in questionnaires Q1 and Q2

	Data collected
Q1	– Subject characteristics (age, qualification, professional experience)
	– Typical role of subject in the software engineering process
	– The subject's knowledge of the concepts of the approach and the ACUE support environment (pre-test, based on the introductory material supplied)
Q2	– The subject's knowledge of the concepts of the approach and the ACUE support environment (post-test, based on the scenario-guided interaction with the support environment)
	– The subject's assessment of the usefulness and ease-of-use of the support environment

9.1.5 Tasks

Under real-life work conditions, the different groups of subjects would perform different types of tasks. Therefore to study the acceptance of the ACUE support environment under as realistic conditions as possible, different usage scenarios were developed for each user group.

The scenarios were written in natural language. They defined the role of the subject in the scenario and contained the tasks to be solved. All scenarios were embedded in a cover story that set a common background for all scenarios.

Scenario S0 was identical for all user groups. In S0, the subjects were allowed to freely explore all components of the ACUE support environment. The other scenario tasks differed among the user groups. They are summarized in Table 9.3.

Table 9.3 Description of the Tasks

Scenario	Tasks
NE-S1	Find an explanation of the term "usability engineering". Mark the section for later exploration.
NE-S2	Find an introductory article about evaluation and testing. Review the material supplied.
NE-S3	Open the method kit for the DIGital project. Find and open the method package on heuristic evaluation.
SE-S1	Browse all method packages available for the DIGital project. Find and display a package on heuristic evaluation. Assess the acceptance of the heuristic evaluation method.
SE-S2	Comment on the "heuristic evaluation" method. Edit the method. Extend the method package with a checklist.
SE-S3	Create a new method package. Fill the package with the raw input material provided. Specify the meta-data of the method's context model. Link the package to related packages.
UE-S1	Create a new method kit for the PORTAL project. Choose a context model and specify the project characteristics via the context model. Choose appropriate method packages based on the provided project characteristics. Trigger the generation of a hypermedia workspace for the method kit.
UE-S2	Manage access to the method kit for the PORTAL project. Invite project team members. Manage access levels of project team members.

9.1.6 Procedure

Prior to the evaluation sessions, all the subjects received introductory materials in electronic format that briefly described the concepts of the ACUE approach and the components of the support environment. Subjects who had no access to the materials prior to the evaluation were given the opportunity to study print-outs.

Each evaluation session started with a short introduction of the participants, the procedure, and the objectives of the study. The subjects were informed that the goal of the evaluation was to assess the usefulness of the approach and not the capabilities of the participants and that all data would be treated confidentially.

After the introduction, the pre-test (Q1) questionnaire was handed out. Next, the tasks to be solved were handed out in the form of scenarios. Scenario S0 was performed by all participants in order to promote a free exploration of the system. The time for S0 was limited to 20 minutes. Next, the group-specific scenarios were handed out to the subjects. No time limit was set for the completion of these tasks. The subjects were encouraged to articulate impressions and problems and think out loud while performing the tasks. After all scenarios were completed, the post-test questionnaire (Q2) was administered. The evaluation concluded with a brief open discussion.

Two observers were involved in each evaluation session. One observer recorded the behavioral data, while the other was responsible for writing down comments made while the subjects were thinking out loud. During the session, the subjects worked on a laptop, with each session lasting roughly two hours. The schedule of a typical evaluation session is provided in Table 9.4.

Table 9.4 Schedule of a typical evaluation session

Time [min.]	Procedure
10	Introduction
15	Administration of questionnaire Q1
20	Free exploration of the support environment (Scenario S0)
50	Performance of scenarios 1–3 according to the subject group
15	Administration of questionnaire Q2
10	Open discussion

9.2 Results of the Studies and Recommendations

The qualitative effects analysis shows that the approach is most strongly accepted by the main target group of the support environment, the UE group. However, the support environment also received higher-than-average ratings from the other subject groups. A detailed description of the results is provided in the following sections.

9.2.1 Characteristics of the Subject Groups

The characteristics of the group members regarding age and professional experience are set out in Table 9.5.

Table 9.5 Characteristics of subject groups

		New employees	Software engineers	Usability engineers	Overall
Age [Years]	Mean	24	34	37	32
	Range	20–29	22–50	23–52	20–52
Average professional experience [years]		1.5	7.5	8.8	6.5
Average time in present function [years]		1.2	5.9	4.8	4.6

The question on the project activities performed by the subjects in their professional roles revealed ten activities. Although showing slightly different distributions, the same activities were identified by all three groups.

The three most-cited activities were programming, user interface development and system maintenance. Figures 9.1, 9.2 and 9.3 illustrate the distribution of the subjects' main tasks across the three subject groups.

The variance in functions and core tasks in the subject profiles reflects the project-dependent deployment of the persons, i.e. tasks are assigned to project team members depending on the requirements of the project. It seems to be rare for subjects to specialize in just a single professional area in the organizations examined.

It is concluded that the population examined in this study is typical for these areas as far as age and professional experience are concerned. As they do not show any unusual distribution, the results are expected to be generalizable from this perspective.

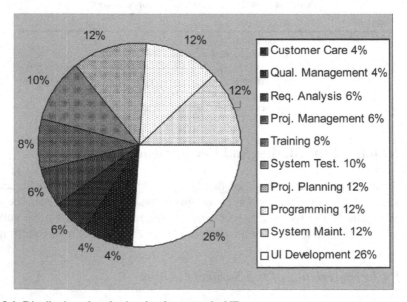

Fig. 9.1 Distribution of professional tasks across the NE group

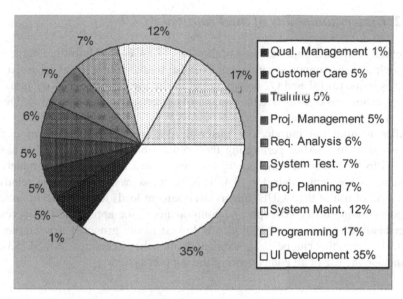

Fig. 9.2 Distribution of professional tasks across the SE group

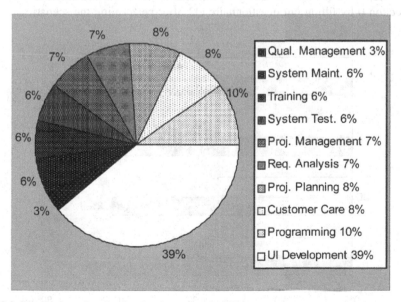

Fig. 9.3 Distribution of professional tasks across the UE group

9.2.2 Understandability of the Proposed ACUE

As set out above, the understanding of the Adoption-Centric Usability Engineering approach and the support environment ProUSE by the subjects was measured via the questionnaires Q1 and Q2 before and after the use of the support system. The understanding was measured as the number of correct answers in the knowledge test parts of the questionnaires.

After reading the introductory material, the average percentage of correct answers was 36%. After performing the scenario-based tasks, this value almost doubled to 63%. The performance of the groups and the overall performance of the subjects are depicted in Fig. 9.4. This figure shows that even the relatively short time of use of the ACUE support environment leads to a significant increase in understanding of the concepts and components of the approach. The increased understanding of the overall approach is lowest in the group of new employees (NE). However, this can be easily explained since their scenarios (NE-S1–S3) did not include the use of all components of the support system.

9.2.3 ACUE Perceived Usefulness

For the qualitative effects analysis, subjects were asked to assess the properties of the ACUE support environments along the dimensions for perceived usefulness defined in Section 0 by filling out questionnaire Q2 after performing the scenario-specific

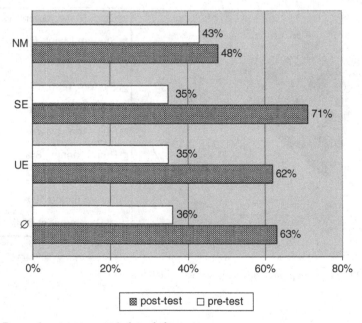

Fig. 9.4 Pre- and post-test scores in knowledge tests

tasks. For this reason, questionnaire Q2 included a number of items to be rated on a five-level Likert scale (Judd et al., 1991) for the perceived usefulness of the approach (compatibility with daily practice, usefulness as a tool, support of working tasks, increase in knowledge, and increased efficiency of UE).

Figure 9.5 presents the results of the qualitative effects analysis. The bars represent ratings of the assessment dimensions. The mean ratings are calculated for each dimension and grouped by subject group. A rating of 1 indicates a strong disagreement while a rating of 5 indicates a strong agreement.

The results indicate that the approach and its support environment are generally assessed by all groups as higher-than-average on usefulness and reasonableness. All subjects seemed to highly appreciate the potential of the approach for increasing their knowledge of software engineering methods.

The dimension of task support received the highest scores from the UE group. This corresponds to the pre-configuration of the support environment with usability engineering methods and the subjects' role as usability engineers. It can be

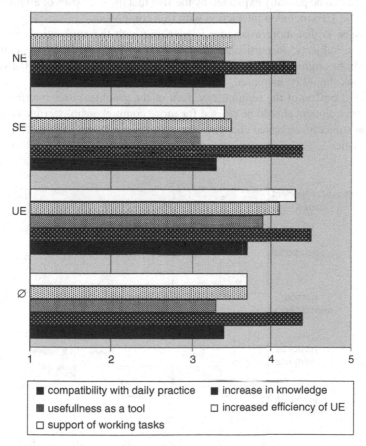

Fig. 9.5 Results of the qualitative effects analysis

concluded that the assessment of this dimension by the other groups could be further enhanced by integrating software engineering methods for other areas such as requirements engineering or methods for enhancing programmer productivity into the method repository of the ACUE support environment. This result underpins the necessity to provide benefits for all groups of project personnel involved in process improvement activities.

9.2.4 ACUE Perceived Ease-of-Use

The behavioral data and user comments recorded during task performance suggest that there is potential for improving the usability of the support environment. The distribution of usability issues identified by subjects across the client components of the support environment are set out in Fig. 9.6. Most improvement suggestions were related to the components for process guidance and adoption-centric decision support. The high number of usability issues identified for the process guidance component can be partially explained by the fact that the scenarios of all user groups (NE, SE and UE) included interaction with this component.

One issue is that more assistance in working with the applications is appreciated by the subjects. In particular, novice users could profit from concepts such as wizards to augment context capturing. Moreover the consistency between the applications should be increased.

Finally the parts of the terminology used in the graphical user interfaces of the support environment should be revised for more comprehensible terms. One example is that subjects suggested changing the term "project context model" to "project characteristics".

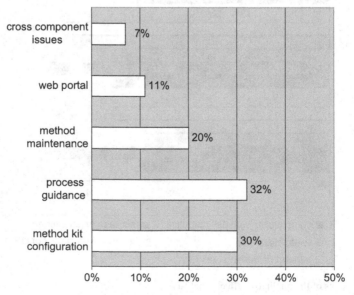

Fig. 9.6 Distribution of usability issues

9.3 Interviewee Statements on the Practiced Software Development Process

9.3.1 Overview

Questionnaire sections on the subjects' development processes aimed at examining from which sources the subjects drew their knowledge about software development processes, which process models were used, which usability engineering methods were used and the subjects' roles as project team members.

This data is interesting for a number of reasons. First, one of the assumptions of this work is that development organizations are largely practicing highly diverse development processes. The data allow us to test this assumption. Based on this assumption of diverse processes, the Adoption-Centric Usability Engineering framework proposed the concept of a configurable usability engineering method kit, which can be adapted to specific development projects.

Another interesting question with respect to this work is from which source the project teams acquire their process knowledge and if they already have process support tools in use.

9.3.2 Knowledge About the Software Development Process

The different subject groups drew their knowledge about software development processes from different sources. The subjects of the SE and UE groups largely relied on the knowledge that they acquired in their professional experience. In all three subject groups, knowledge acquired during the course of studies played a prominent role. Professional development seems to be relevant only for the SE group.

The distribution of the different sources of knowledge about software development processes over the different subject groups is depicted in Fig. 9.7. The vertical axis indicates how often the respective source was identified by a subject group.

9.3.3 Process Models Used by Subjects

Only 27% of the subjects stated that they followed a specified process model in their project teams. The questionnaire allowed freely naming any process model. Figure 9.8 shows the number of citations for the named process models. It shows that most subjects (31 of 44 persons) made no statements. Five subjects stated that they used a company specific process model and four subjects followed the V-Model [IABG]in their projects.

These statements might merely confirm that questions without predefined answers are seldom completed by the subjects. It is thus possible that far more process models were applied in the project teams than were articulated.

However, if we accept these results as the real situation in the organizations, the comparison with the results described in the previous chapter allows interesting

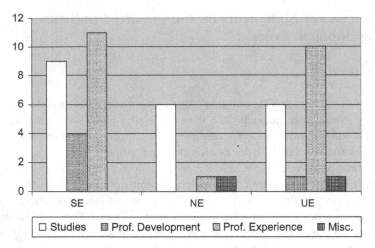

Fig. 9.7 Sources of knowledge about software development processes

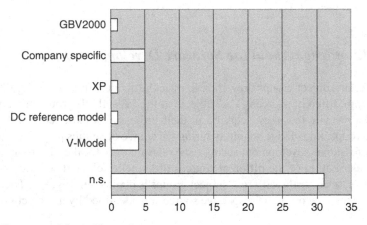

Fig. 9.8 Process models used by project teams

conclusions. On the one hand the majority of interviewees could not name a process model as the basis for their overall software development process. On the other hand the development team members were able to sketch their development process at the abstraction level of method kits, including phases and main process activities. This could indicate that usability engineering method kits are in fact a useful abstraction level for development teams for reflecting their existing development processes and understanding usability engineering methodologies, while over-specified process models are rarely rigorously practiced and are largely unknown to development teams. However, such a conclusion requires more thoroughly investigating the over-all software development process.

9.3.4 The Usability Engineering Process

As indicated in Table 9.6, usability engineering is judged by all subject groups as being of higher-than-average relevancy on a five-level Likert scale (1 = I totally disagree, 5 = I totally agree). However, the table also shows that knowledge about the methods and the support for usability engineering is not sufficient. This underlines the large demand for a tool such as ProUSE.

Subjects' knowledge on the topic of usability engineering varied greatly before the test. As expected, the UE subject group was highly familiar with this topic, whereas only 60% of the NE and SE subject groups were familiar with it. This indicates that it cannot be assumed that usability engineering is known by typical computer science professionals (The subjects of the NE group are largely computer science students).

Only eight subjects (27%) used a usability engineering process model similar to the model presented in the introductory material. Five subjects of this group belonged to the UE group.

Regarding the question on which alternative UE approaches are used, only a few subjects gave an answer. The answers contained no specific UE techniques but rather statements such as "trial and error" or "learning by doing". However, these results might not be representative, as again no predefined answers are offered to the subjects and the subjects are possibly not able to remember the terms for the models used.

After the study, the usability engineering reference model of ProUSE was presented to the subjects. They were asked with which process activities they were familiar. The following table makes clear that the subjects' state of knowledge varied considerably across the subject groups and specific process activities. Table 9.7 only contains the three process steps with the most and the least nominations.

9.3.5 Subjects' Roles as Project Team Members

Thirty two of forty four subjects held a specific role within their project teams. As could be expected, this especially applied to the software engineer (SE) and usability

Table 9.6 Assessment of the relevancy of usability engineering methods

	NE	SE	UE	Av.
Overall utility of UE methods	3,4	2,9	3,4	3,2
Usability is supported by my development environment	2,5	1,3	2,5	1,9
I would use UE methods even if I have to meet a deadline	2,7	2,6	2,5	2,9
UE methods require knowledge that is available in the development team.	2,9	3,1	2,9	2,7
In my working area UE methods are deployed.	2,2	2,7	3,5	2,9
With more help I would deploy UE methods during development.	3,9	4,0	4,3	4,0
I think the deployment of UE methods in the development process is reasonable.	4,4	4,1	4,5	4,3

Table 9.7 Familiarity of subjects with UE method (highest and lowest familiarity topics)

Process activity	NE	SE	UE	Av.
Task analysis	70	57	62	63
Capture change requests	70	67	46	63
As-is analysis	70	43	69	58
Workflow reengineering	10	19	31	21
Manage release change	10	14	31	19
Usability training	10	5	39	16

engineer (UE) subject groups, whereas new employees were not yet firmly assigned to a project team or were still exploring different working areas. The most cited role is the role of the programmer. Figure 9.9 shows all roles named by the subjects. Clearly defined roles seem to be rare. More often professional tasks and roles were mixed.

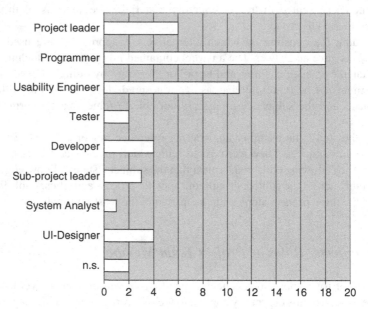

Fig. 9.9 Roles named by subjects

The number of roles held by each subject within a project team varied between zero and three roles. Members of the SE and UE groups mostly held one or two roles. New employees often do not claim to be assigned a role.

Part IV
ACUE in Software Engineering: Current Stage and Perspectives

Chapter 10
ACUE and the Existing Software Engineering Methodologies

Adoption-Centric Usability Engineering (ACUE) has connections with a number of fields such as tools for working with guidelines, empirical software engineering, software engineering process improvement and organizational learning. In this section the principles and elements of the Adoption-Centric Usability Engineering approach are compared with other approaches. The goal of this comparison is to illustrate the differences of the approach developed in this work as compared to other approaches. We also indicate how the Adoption-Centric Usability Engineering approach can supplement existing approaches.

10.1 USEPacks Versus Other Approaches for Reusing UE Knowledge

In the previous chapters, Usability Engineering Experience Packages (USEPacks) were proposed as an alternative for capturing and deploying usability engineer (UE) knowledge in the software engineering process. In this chapter, the advantages and drawbacks of USEPacks are discussed as compared to other approaches. In particular, we compare them to the techniques for capturing design knowledge including guidelines (Smith and Mosier, 1986); (Vanderdonckt, 1999), interaction patterns (Brighton Usability Group, 1999); (Coram and Lee, 2002); (Tidwell, 1999); (Welie, 1999), and claims (Rosson et al., 2001).

Interaction patterns are based on existing design artifacts. Advantages and drawbacks of a design solution are recorded in a pattern to support designers in reasoning about the use of a pattern. The ultimate goal of the pattern community is to create a pattern language, which is a set of interrelated patterns that cover a wide variety of systems, users, domains and design problems. The aim of patterns is to systemize the design process and stimulate reuse of successful design solutions.

Prima facie, the most obvious difference between USEPacks and interaction patterns is that USEPacks focus on knowledge about processes and methods instead of specific design solutions. As with almost all approaches for integrating UE knowledge into development processes, interaction patterns assume that a usability engineering process is available and established in the development team. Likewise,

A. Seffah, E. Metzker, *Adoption-centric Usability Engineering*,
DOI 10.1007/978-1-84800-019-3_10, © Springer-Verlag London Limited 2009

they assume that human-factors experts who can make use of such knowledge are available and established in the development team.

To make use of patterns in the design phase, the development team has to perform at least a basic analysis of user tasks and user attributes. Without such an analysis, a pattern-augmented design process lacks necessary information for an informed selection of patterns. But the results of the previous evaluation chapter, which support the working hypotheses behind ACUE indicate that the assumption of the existence of even rudimentary usability engineering processes is often unjustified in software development projects. USEPacks try to bridge this gap, as they provide knowledge on UE techniques and utilities to enable development teams to more effectively deploy UE in their development processes.

Claims extend patterns by additionally providing theories for each design artifact, which justify the use of the respective solution. Furthermore, a scenario provides context information to understand under which constraints the solution of a claim can be applied. The author sees claims as a contribution to a more systematic way of teaching user interface design.

Given the high volatility of the corporate knowledge of design rationales, it would be valuable to investigate the costs and benefits of capturing, maintaining and using detailed design rationales.

The more important feature of USEPacks is that they can cope with the uncertain validity of the knowledge that they capture. Most of the existing approaches assume the a priori validity of the knowledge captured.

Another difference that distinguishes USEPacks from other techniques for capturing UE knowledge is their formalized context profiles. The formalized context profile allows the development of similarity measures that enable a computer aided matching of project characteristics with appropriate UE process knowledge captured as USEPacks.

Together with the Adoption-Centric Usability Engineering approach, USEPacks provide mechanisms to increase the reliability of the captured knowledge. This is achieved by continuously evaluating and improving the captured UE knowledge based on feedback from project teams who deploy USEPacks.

The consistency of current pattern collections could be increased if the strengths and weaknesses of patterns were described in a more formal way, similar to the context profiles of USEPacks. In addition, the confidence in pattern-based user interface design approaches could be increased by submitting patterns to a systematic evaluation process which examines the appropriateness of applying a pattern in a given context in relation to the pattern's strengths and weaknesses. A support system similar to ProUSE which supports such efforts could be a first step toward creating a pattern language for user interface design.

10.2 ProUSE Versus Other Tools for Reusing UE Knowledge

A large number of tools has been developed for supporting the integration of UE knowledge in software development processes. Examples are Master-Mind

(Stirewalt et al., 1997), MOBI-D (Puerta and Maulsby, 1997), FUSE (Lonczewski and Schreiber, 1996), Tadeus (Forbrig and Dittmar, 1999), Expose (Gorny, 1995), and Sherlock (Grammenos et al., 2000). Again, a classification according to user interface development philosophies is useful (see Chapter 2).

Table 10.1 overviews the approaches that are well documented in the literature. These approaches and the ProUSE support tool for ACUE are classified according to their development philosophy and according to the phases of the development process that they support.

In the following section, two of these approaches, GUIDE and Sherlock, are described in more detail. GUIDE is described because it comes closest to some concepts that can also be found in ProUSE. Sherlock receives attention because it is one of the best examples of a tight integration of user interface design knowledge into the development process.

Sherlock

Sherlock (Grammenos et al., 2000) is a user interface guideline management system that assists developers in usability inspections. It supports the design team during early phases of prototype development of interactive systems. Sherlock is operated by a usability analyst who inspects early versions of a prototype for compliance with a defined set of rules.

Sherlock is implemented as a client server system. The client is a plug-in to the Visual Basic integrated development environment (IDE). The server stores

Table 10.1 Tools supporting different user interface development approaches

Process Phase		User Interface Development Philosophy	
		Engineering Approach	Technologist Approach
	Planning	◎ ●	
	Req. Anal.	● ⊙	
	Design	◎ ●	⊙ ✕ ✧ ◆ □
	Implem.	●	⊙ ✳ ✧ ◆ □
	Testing	●	✳ ◆
	Deploy.	●	

Legend:

◎ GUIDE	● ProUSE
◆ Mastermind	✳ Sherlock
⊙ Mobi-D	□ FUSE
✧ Tadeus	✕ Expose

guideline-related knowledge and manages updates of the rule base. The inspection rules stored on the server are implemented as dynamic link library (DLL) modules.

The client is used to evaluate user interfaces developed in Visual Basic and to review the evaluation results. Knowledge regarding specific inspection rules can be accessed and data about previous evaluation sessions can be viewed.

A central advantage of Sherlock is the tight integration with the most important tool of every developer, the integrated development environment (IDE). The system provides design and inspection functionality extending beyond guideline access. For example, recommendations from the assistance system can be directly propagated to the actual implementation and need no prior interpretation by the developer. Thus, the effort of adopting the tool seems to be reasonably low for developers.

From a process point of view, Sherlock provides the benefit that the technique of usability inspection based on heuristics is tightly integrated with the task of developing the user interface. The approach therefore has the potential to unburden developers from tedious and time-consuming usability inspections that deal with issues of inconsistency and style guide conformity. Usability experts are able to focus on their core activities such as task analysis and usability testing.

Sherlock also supports process improvements on the organizational level by offering functions for report generation. The reports provide descriptions of each rule violation detected, the respective guideline and how the same problem was solved in the past. Figure 10.1 portrays a sample scenario of the deployment of Sherlock by usability experts, programmers and designers.

However, Sherlock cannot completely replace expert evaluations or usability tests with users. With an optimal rule set, Sherlock can only detect violations of guidelines that focus on attributes of a single screen of an application. In the best case Sherlock can perform as well as an expert evaluator who focuses on the static usability attributes of a GUI. The Sherlock system is constrained by the limits of automated user interface evaluation, which have been investigated and are well documented in the literature (Reed et al., 1999), (Tetzlaff and Schwartz, 1991); (Vanderdonckt, 1999).

However, tools like Sherlock have the potential to support compliance with corporate style guides and eliminate problems of design inconsistency which are otherwise tedious to spot and correct.

GUIDE

GUIDE (Guidelines for Usability through Interface Development Experiences) was developed to support creation and maintenance of online usability guidelines (Henninger, 2000). Developers are stepped through a process that supports the utilization of usability guidelines in software development projects. The basic concepts of GUIDE are a guideline hierarchy, cases and rules.

At the beginning of a project or during development, GUIDE supports team members in eliciting the characteristics of the design problem at hand. GUIDE uses rules to match the design problem to the most appropriate guidelines.

Rules are represented as question-answer pairs in a decision tree structure. Answering a question results in the selection of a set of relevant guidelines.

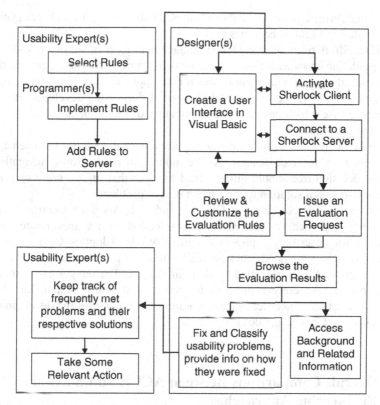

Fig. 10.1 A sample scenario of using Sherlock

Furthermore, the selected answer determines the next question that is asked in the problem elicitation process. By answering questions, developers navigate through the decision tree that is created in the problem elicitation process. The result of this problem elicitation process is a set of design guidelines that is tailored to the specific needs of the design problem.

In a joint review process, developers and human-factors experts decide which of the selected guidelines need to be followed and which are not applicable in the current project. Also new guidelines can be created if necessary. If deviations from assigned guidelines are required, the reviewers must decide whether changes are necessary in the rules or guidelines.

The way individual projects achieve guideline performance is documented in "cases". A case is assigned to a guideline for each project that has applied the guideline.

Preliminary evaluations show that there are some issues which hamper the successful adoption of GUIDE in practice. One problem described by Henninger is the high effort of creating and maintaining meaningful rule sets (Henninger, 2000). Small changes in guidelines and rules often require restructuring the whole decision tree. With a growing number of rules, a better support for checking consistency of rules and actions becomes necessary.

GUIDE differs from other guideline management tools in the process for evolving the guideline knowledge base. An organization starts with a set of general design guidelines and specific widget guidelines for the applications typically developed in that organization. Whenever a guideline is used during the development of user interfaces, a case which describes the application of the guideline is recorded and attached to the guideline.

The cases associated with a guideline capture how that guideline has been applied to different user interface designs. As the number of cases grows, navigating the guideline decision tree should directly lead to cases that offer a more appropriate and context-relevant solution to the current design problem.

A major difference between GUIDE and the Adoption-Centric Usability Engineering approach in ProUSE is the selection of an appropriate type of knowledge for describing a project situation. While Adoption-Centric Usability Engineering uses aggregated data from the feedback of project teams, GUIDE relies on human-created rules provided by domain experts. The danger exists that such human-created rules correspond more to the untested assumptions of the domain experts than actual project feedback, a common problem with the development of methodologies (Cockburn, 2001).

10.3 Overall Comparisons Between ACUE and Software Engineering Approaches

In relation to tool-based support, a large number of tools have been developed for supporting the use of guidelines for generating and evaluating user interfaces. Examples of these approaches are discussed above and can be found in Table 10.1. The limits of such approaches are well documented in the literature (Reed et al., 1999); (Tetzlaff and Schwartz, 1991); (Vanderdonckt, 1999).

To the knowledge of the author, no special tools are available to support the creation and maintenance of style guides. Standard word processors are still the main utility for working with style guides. This is especially interesting as many UE approaches recommend the use of style guides during development.

Tools to support working with HCI patterns still focus on making sets of patterns available on the Internet. Approaches for integrating interaction patterns into existing integrated development environments (IDE) are still missing. A number of problems seem to hamper the successful operationalization of interaction patterns. One issue is that it is still unclear in which activities of development processes interaction patterns should be integrated. Should patterns be applied during requirements analysis or design? How can patterns be constructively used during the development process?

It is unknown if and how patterns can be further formalized to prepare them for computational support. Even creating a common classification system for pattern strengths seems to be a very ambitious goal. Useful dimensions for such a classification system have not yet been found. New paradigms have to be developed to map developers' design requirements to existing solutions captured as patterns.

To the knowledge of the author, ProUSE is the only tool that supports UE from a process-centered point of view. ProUSE does not assume the existence of a UE process in a development organization; instead it provides configurable UE method kits. Method kits are adaptable based on project experiences and feedback from project teams.

ProUSE supports the collection, aggregation and exploitation of data on the usefulness and ease-of-use of UE methods as perceived by project teams. ProUSE aims at fostering an organizational learning process that leads to greater confidence for selecting appropriate UE methods.

As can be seen in Table 10.1, almost no approaches are available that combine any two of the user interface design philosophies, such as the engineering approach and the technologist approach.

A first step was attempted in the EMBASSI project (BMBF, 2000). ProUSE was integrated with a tool from the cognitive psychology research stream of human – computer interaction, GUIDEAS (Guidance for Developing Assistance) (Köppen, 2002). GUIDEAS assists developers in requirements analysis for assistance systems. Based on a set of empirically derived questions, criteria and rules, GUIDEAS recommends certain types of assistance functions for a system under development.

10.4 ACUE in Relation to Process Improvement Approaches

Recently the concept of process maturity was introduced to the field of usability engineering. (International Organization for Standardization, 2000). The rationale behind usability maturity models is that there are direct dependencies among (1) an organization's capability to tailor its UE processes according to various constraints, (2) the quality of the development process performed and (3) the quality in use of the interactive software system. Generally an organization has reached the maximum usability maturity level when it is able to perform, control, tailor and continuously improve its usability engineering activities.

The ProUSE approach as discussed above is geared to support software engineering organizations in reaching high usability maturity levels. At a low usability maturity level, development organizations can use the experience base as a repository for base practices which are found in the initial set of USEPacks and which enable the engineering teams to deploy those base practices. By applying the base practices in various projects, development organizations are able to derive USEPacks that capture project constraints such as the size of the development team or the available budget.

In this way, an organization develops a set of more contextualized methods for each base practice, which will enable the organization to control its usability engineering activities. This means the appropriate method can be selected based on given resource constraints from the set of USEPacks available in the method pool.

By applying these controlled methods in new projects, the organization collects experience on how to apply the available methods in different domains or for different technologies. By capturing these experiences in more contextualized USEPacks and feeding them into the experience base, the organization increases its capability to tailor the set of available methods to the current development context. For example, the organization will be able to have an optimized set of usability engineering methods for developing intelligent assistants with the avatar technology using a medium size budget with a small development team. By evaluating and refining each method after applying it, a continuous improvement process is triggered.

Houdek (1999) developed a classification scheme for software quality improvement approaches. Figure 10.2 shows an excerpt of this classification scheme that highlights the two most influential streams of software quality improvement approaches – the bottom-up and top-down software process improvement paradigms – and shows how Adoption-Centric Usability Engineering is classified according to this scheme.

Both the bottom-up and top-down approaches focus on improving the quality of software products by improving the underlying development process.

However, top-down approaches like SPICE (ISO-SPICE, 1998) or the Capability Maturity Model (CMM) (Humphrey, 1990) propose an ideal software development process. The underlying assumption is that adopting an ideal software development process results in producing higher quality products with higher reliability.

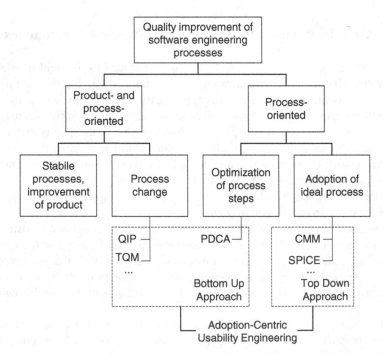

Fig. 10.2 Classification of ACUE in relation to other Software Process Improvement (SPI) approaches

Bottom-up approaches such as the Quality Improvement Paradigm (QIP) (Basili et al., 1994) are based on the plan-do-check-act (PDCA) cycle developed by Shewart (1931). PDCA is based on the paradigm of incremental improvement of practiced processes. In a planning phase, the improvement goals, activities, and appropriate measures are defined. In the implementation phase (Do), the plan is executed in a target environment. The success of the improvement activities is examined based on previously defined criteria and the measured data. Based on this analysis, actions are taken to improve the process.

As indicated in Fig. 10.2, the Adoption-Centric Usability Engineering approach is a combination of the bottom-up and top-down process improvement paradigms. It is a top-down approach as it provides process guidance via the UE method kit. After configuration, the project-specific instance of the UE method kit represents a form of ideal process for assuring the usability of the system under development.

On the other hand, ACUE is also a bottom-up approach. Data on the usefulness of deployed UE techniques is continually collected within development projects and exploited for process optimization. Experiences collected in projects are systematically recorded to extend the ideal process.

10.5 ACUE as an Approach to Improve Research Utilization

ACUE can be interpreted as a contribution for overcoming the problem of research utilization in software engineering in general. Research utilization is defined as the process of using research findings to guide practice. In other words, this is the "process by which scientifically produced knowledge is transferred to practice" (Shrivastava and Mitroff, 1984).

The problem of the still low impact of empirical research on software engineering practice has been widely recognized in the community: "defining and executing studies that change how software development is done – is the greatest challenge facing empirical researchers" (Perry et al., 2000).

The problem of insufficient and unsystematic research utilization is also recognized in established scientific fields such as medicine. Paradoxically, one issue that seems to contribute to the problem is the large amount of scientific output. In medicine, for example, the number of bio-medical journals has doubled since 1970. To keep up with current publications in general medicine alone would mean reading 19 articles per day, 365 days per year. However, clinicians admit to spending just 1 hour per week reading journals.

Unsystematic research utilization in medicine has resulted in clinical decisions that are largely based on anecdotal clinical experience rather than available scientific evidence. Motivated by cost and quality issues, demands have been raised to base medical decisions on so called evidence-based guidelines. An evidence based medicinal guideline is defined by the evidence source equation:

$$Evidence - based guideline = clinical expertise + patient preferences$$
$$+ scientific findings$$

USEPacks can be interpreted as a step toward evidence-based guidelines for the deployment of software engineering methods. They can incorporate scientific findings in the form of software engineering method descriptions. The adoption-centric approach developed in this work proposes to evaluate such findings within the software engineering lifecycle and get feedback from project teams. The ACUE approach provides means to enhance theories of software engineering methods by project experiences and acquire and exploit information on the usefulness and ease-of-use of software engineering methods as perceived by project teams.

The concepts and tools of the ACUE approach allow combining and operationalizing such scientific and experience-based information to improve confidence in selecting appropriate methods for software development projects. ACUE has the potential to be as effective in showing that certain proven methods are underused as in showing that ineffective approaches are overused – thereby contributing to an evidence-based utilization of software engineering research.

10.6 ACUE and Agile Process Concepts

A number of modern software development methodologies such as extreme programming (XP) (Beck, 2000), Crystal (Cockburn, 2001), Scrum (Beedle et al., 1999), and Dynamic System Development Method (DSDM) (Stapleton, 1997) are subsumed under the term of "agile methodologies". The common denominator of these methodologies is summarized in four central statements of the agile manifesto:

- Individuals and interactions over processes and tools
- Working software over comprehensive documentation
- Customer collaboration over contract negotiation
- Responding to change over following a plan

While strongly focusing on software development issues such as incremental releases, programmer productivity and minimal documentation, agile methodologies also address some aspects of process improvement. In this section we will examine how the agile concepts of "methodology-per-project" and "just-in-time methodology construction" relate to certain ideas in Adoption-Centric Usability Engineering.

"Methodology-per-project" simply addresses the problem that a single software development methodology does not fit all projects. A software development methodology must be appropriate for the given project characteristics. Cockburn suggests that for each new project, a base methodology should be adapted to reflect the needs of the current project. The technique proposed for adapting a methodology is called "methodology tuning". In a methodology tuning workshop, the project team selects an existing base methodology and adapts it to its needs. The resulting methodology is called the "starter methodology".

Cockburn has developed a set of starter methodologies – the family of Crystal methodologies – that can be deployed in projects with certain project characteristics. The Crystal methodologies are classified according to two project characteristics: first, the number of people involved and second, the degree of safety-criticality of the software to be developed in the project.

After each increment, a "reflection workshop" is performed by the project team in which the starter methodology is analyzed and changed if necessary.

In Adoption-Centric Usability Engineering, some of the concepts just described can be found in a more formalized way. For example, the idea of a pool of usability engineering techniques from which an appropriate subset can be selected to form the usability engineering process of a new project can be interpreted as an example of "just-in-time method construction". An ACUE method kit with its process phases, activities and related USEPacks can be understood as a "starter methodology".

Whereas in Crystal only two dimensions of methodology selection are described – size of project staff and system criticality – the ACUE context profiles offer a more formal, comprehensive and flexible way of method classification.

The agile idea of method analysis and adaptation can be found in the method assessment sessions of ACUE. Again ACUE offers more formal concepts: method assessments are conducted by using the clearly defined rating scales of acceptance models. Changes to methods can be captured by modifying existing USEPacks or creating new USEPacks. Changed or new methods can be directly adopted in the current project but are also available in subsequent projects. Furthermore, the formalized method assessment mechanism allows an automatic adaptation of a USEPack context profile.

In summary, ACUE can be interpreted as an agile usability engineering meta-model. ACUE provides semi-formal mechanisms to effectively support agile process concepts such as just-in-time method construction, starter methodologies and reflection workshops.

Chapter 11
Conclusion and Perspectives

In the current shift to mobile, persuasive and immersive applications, new forms of user interfaces are emerging which lead to new development challenges and methodologies. This concluding chapter reviews the fundamentals of Adoption-Centric Usability Engineering (ACUE) while discussing how the approach can evolve and how it can be tailored to the specific requirements of an organization or a new type project.

11.1 Conclusion and Limitations

This book describes the results of a long-term research work that has a relatively large scope: an approach for improving the integration of usability engineering methods into software development processes. A software environment was developed and a comprehensive empirical study was conducted to evaluate the acceptance of the approach by software engineering practitioners.

As discussed in Section 11.1, the integration problem is multidisciplinary and therefore it is a very difficult issue to assess empirically. For this broad scope it has not been possible to provide equal coverage, formality, and empirical evaluation to all aspects of the concepts that have been developed. Instead we focused on four fundamental concerns. These were, to:

1. Develop concepts that address the problem at levels that have been underestimated by previous usability engineering methods (See Chapter)
2. Formalize the proposed approach so far as to make them computationally manageable
3. Operationalize the approach via a support tool that embodies the central concepts
4. Examine the acceptance of the developed concepts by practitioners while measuring the potential impacts of the approach and get feedback for improvement

At an empirical level, the constructs presented here have not yet been broadly evaluated. In particular, the empirical studies presented in Section 11.3 have been conducted in industrial settings. While this context provided valuable information, the practical constraints and difficulties have limited the number of feasible study types

A. Seffah, E. Metzker, *Adoption-centric Usability Engineering*,
DOI 10.1007/978-1-84800-019-3_11, © Springer-Verlag London Limited 2009

and designs. We believe that the challenges of introducing, evaluating and improving usability engineering techniques can only be examined in practice; it is proposed that such industry-based approach is the correct way to study these phenomena.

Even though we have reported on empirical evaluations of the approach, the number of available studies limits the generalizability of the results. These findings should be confirmed by a series of additional studies to examine if the approach can be successfully adopted in practice.

11.2 Some Avenues to Explore

The elements of the Adoption-Centric Usability Engineering must be understood as a first step toward the ultimate goal of understanding and exploiting the complex dependencies between (1) specific software development methods and the usability engineering toolbox, (2) the characteristics of projects and (3) the acceptance or rejection of usability engineer (UE) methods by development teams. Several aspects of the framework are not fully mature yet and pose questions for further research. There are no limits on the number of studies that could be performed on the framework as well as the support tool.

The ProUSE support tool which embodies the concept of the framework can easily be adapted to handle context factors and acceptance models other than those presented in this book. One of these aspects is the acceptance model which is deployed for assessing usability engineering methods.

The acceptance model used here involves the acceptance factors "ease-of-use" and "usefulness", which are derived from theories of technology acceptance. A range of further candidate models could be deployed to measure the acceptance of methods in the Adoption-Centric Usability Engineering framework. Examples of such models are "perceived characteristics of innovating" (PCI) (Moore and Benbasat, 1991) and "theory of planned behavior" (Ajzen and Madden, 1986). Future studies could be performed to examine the appropriateness of these models for explaining the acceptance of development methods. These studies could be used to improve the acceptance model used in the Adoption-Centric Usability Engineering approach.

In addition, the number and type of context factors to be used in context profiles requires further study. At this point it is not clear which factors are more important: product-oriented context factors such as the application type and application domain or team-oriented factors such as experience and spatial distribution of the development team. This question can only be answered by applying the approach in practice and analyzing the resulting data.

A further rewarding direction for future research would be to examine how process- and method-oriented tools such as ProUSE could be more tightly integrated with tools such as integrated development environments.

The most obvious missing link in the results presented in this research is a long-term study in which the Adoption-Centric Usability Engineering approach is applied to a number of projects in one or more software development organizations. The goal of such a study would be to examine how successfully the ACUE approach contributes to the adoption of UE processes and techniques.

Although the degree of adoption cannot be directly measured, ACUE provides some starting points to estimate this factor. The data collected on the usefulness of UE techniques provides information on how often and how successfully UE techniques have been deployed in projects. In the ideal case, the data would indicate a progressively increasing acceptance of UE techniques by project teams over time. Furthermore, the data could be analyzed to examine if certain patterns of optimal methods can be detected for defined project configurations. The evaluation of log-files of the support environment could indicate which components and functions of the support environment are frequently used by development teams.

The empirical studies we conducted should be repeated at regular intervals to examine how the acceptance of the ACUE approach evolves over time. The studies described in this book provide an initial assessment of the concepts of the ACUE approach as perceived by practitioners. It is important that these studies be replicated so that the findings and conclusions can be confirmed or revised.

The ACUE approach should ideally be practiced across project boundaries within an organization. The goal is to learn from feedback from different project teams. However, one could also imagine extending this principle by following the example of open source projects.

A community of researchers and practitioners could create and contribute to an open UE methodology project that uses ACUE as a shared framework. Project teams from different companies and research organizations could contribute by providing USEPacks and utility assessments of methods that they deployed in projects. The community would need to collaboratively evolve context profiles and acceptance models. Useful sets of UE methods and best practices could be distilled for relevant project configurations.

Analyzing the accumulated data would make it possible to identify areas that require more research attention. As discussed in section 11.2, such a project could help both researchers and practitioners find their path in the software engineering methodology jungle: The accumulated data could indicate where and why effective methods are underused as well as showing which ineffective approaches are overused.

11.3 A Forum for Cross-Domain Discussion is Needed

The ACUE approach presented in this paper is a masterpiece toward an effective integration and adoption of usability engineering. Yet, the following questions need to be answered as well:

- How can the software engineering lifecycle be re-designed so that end users and usability engineers can participate actively?

- Which usability artifacts are relevant and what are their added values and relationships to software engineering artifacts?
- What are the usability techniques and activities for gathering and specifying these relevant usability artifacts?
- How can these usability artifacts, techniques and activities be presented to software engineers, as well as being integrated in the software development lifecycle in general? What types of notations and tool support are required?

We have seen in Chapter that some artifacts such as use cases and task models are useful in bridging gaps between Human–Computer Interaction (HCI) and software engineer (SE). These boundary objects can serve each discipline in its own work and also act as a communication tool to coordinate work across disciplines. For example, a designer uses patterns to explore design ideas in the space of presentation and navigation; a usability expert uses them to perform an early usability test; a software engineer uses them as part of the specification of the interface code. The patterns perform different functions for each discipline, yet they provide common ground for sharing knowledge.

A forum is therefore required for promoting and improving HCI and usability engineering techniques and software engineering approaches in the two communities. An example of this type of forum would be to explore avenues for:

- Sharing ideas about potential and innovative ways to cross-pollinate the two disciplines
- Disseminating successful and unsuccessful experiences in how to integrate usability into the software engineering lifecycle, in different sizes of organization
- Building a tighter fit between HCI and software engineering practices and research

References

Agyris, C. and Schön, D., "Organizational Learning: A Theory of Action Perspective," in A Review of Literature on Organizational Learning, C. Agyris and D. Schön, Eds. Reading, Massachusetts: Addison-Wesley, 1978, pp. 316–336.

Ajzen, L. and Madden, T., "Prediction of Goal-Directed Behavior: Attitudes, Intention and Perceived Behavioral Control," Experimental Social Psychology, vol. 22, 1986, pp. 453–474.

Artim, J. M., Object Models in User Interface Design: A CHI Workshop. SIGCHI Bulletin, vol. 29, No, October, 1997.

Artim, J. M. and VanHarmelen, M., "Incorporating Work, Process and Task Analysis into Commercial and Industrial Object-Oriented System Development: A CHI Workshop," SIGCHI Bulletin, vol. 30, No. 4, 1998.

Barry, W. B., Philip, N. P., "Understanding and Controlling Software Costs," IEEE Trans. Software Eng. Vol. 14, No. 10, 1988, pp. 1462–1477.

Basili, V. R., Caldiera, G., and Rombach, H. D., "Experience Factory," in Encyclopedia of Software Engineering, vol. 1, J. J. Marciniak, Ed. New York: John Wiley & Sons, 1994a, pp. 528–532.

Basili, V. R., Caldiera, G., and Rombach, H. D., "The Goal-Question-Metric Paradigm," in Encyclopedia of Software Engineering, J. J. Marciniak, Ed. New York: John Wiley & Sons, 1994b.

Basili, V. R., Shull, F., and Lanubile, F., "Building Knowledge Through Families of Experiments," IEEE Transactions on Software Engineering, vol. 25, 1999, pp. 456–473.

Bass, L. and John, B. E., Achieving Usability Through Software Architectural Styles, CHI '00 Extended Abstracts on Human Factors in Computing Systems, The Hague, The Netherlands, April 01–06, 2001,

Bass, L. and John, B., "Linking Usability to Software Architecture Patterns Through General Scenarios," The Journal of Systems and Software, vol. 66, 2003, pp. 187–197. 150 References.

Beck, K., Extreme Programming Explained: Addison Wesley, 2000.

Beedle, M., Devos, M., Sharon, Y., Schwaber, K., and Sutherland, J., "SCRUM: An Extension Pattern Language for Hyper-Productive Software Development," in Pattern Languages of Program Design 4., Software Patterns Series, N. Harrison, B. Foote, and H. Rohnert, Eds. Addison-Wesley, 1999.

Benyon, D. and Macaulay, C., "Scenarios and the HCI-SE Design Problem," Interacting with Computers, vol. 14, 2002, pp. 397–405.

Bevan, N., "Trial Usability Maturity Process – Cost Benefit Analysis," ESPRIT Project 28015 TRUMP 2000.

Beyer, H. and Holtzblatt, K., Contextual Design: Defining Customer-Centered Systems. Morgan Kaufmann Publishers, 1998.

Bias, "Pluralistic Walkthroughs," in Usability Inspection Methods, J. Nielsen and R. L. Mack, Eds. New York: Wiley, 1994.

Billingsley, P. A., "Starting from Scratch: Building a Usability Program at Union Pacific Railroad," Interactions, vol. 2, 1995, pp. 27–30.

Birk, A., Dingsøyr, T., and Stålhane, T., "Post Mortem: Never Leave a Project Without it," IEEE Software, vol. 19, 2002, pp. 43–45.

BMBF, 2000. "EMBASSI," www.embassi.de/estart.html.

Boehm, B. W., "A Spiral Model of Software Development and Enhancement," IEEE Computer, vol. 21, 1988, pp. 61–72.

Boehm, B., "Software Risk Management: Principles and Practices Boehm, B.W. Software," IEEE vol. 8, No. 1, pp. 32–41, January 1991.

Brighton Usability Group, U. o. B., "The Brighton Usability Pattern Collection," 1999. http://www.it.brighton.ac.uk/research/patterns/home.html.

Carey, T., "Commentary on 'Scenarios and Task Analysis' by Dan Diaper," Interacting with Computers, vol. 14, 2002, pp. 411–412.

Carrol, J. M., "Making Use is More Than a Matter of Task Analysis," Interacting with Computers, vol. 14, 2002, pp. 619–627.

Cockburn, A., "Structuring Use Cases with Goals," Journal of Object Oriented Programming, vol. 10, Sept–Oct, 1997.

Cockburn, A., Agile Software Development. Addison Wesley Longman, 2001.

Constantine, L. L. and Lockwood, L. A. D., Software for Use: A Practical Guide to the Models and Methods of Usage-Centered Design. Addison-Wesley, 1999.

Cooper, A., Reimann, R., and Cronin, D. About Face 3: The Essentials of Interaction Design. John Wiley and Sons, 2007.

Coram, T. and Lee, J., "Experiences: A Pattern Language for User Interface Design" http://www.maplefish.com/todd/papers/experiences/Experiences.html 2002.

Davis, F. D., "A Technology Acceptance Model for Empirically Testing New End-User Information Systems: Theory and Results," in MIT Sloan School of Management. Cambridge, MA, USA: MIT Sloan School of Management, 1986.

Davis, F. D., Bagozzi, R. P., and Warshaw, P. R., "User Acceptance of Computer Technology: A Comparison of Two Theoretical Models," Management Science, 1989, pp. 982–1003.

Dayton, T., Mc Farland, A., and Kramer, J., "Bridging User Needs to Object-Oriented GUI Prototypes via Task Object Design," in User Interface Design: Bridging the Gap from User Requirements to Design, L. E. Wood, Ed. Boca Raton, Florida, USA: CRC Press, 1998, pp. 15–56.

Dempster, A. P., "Upper and Lower Probabilities Induced by a Multi-Valued Mapping," Annals of Mathematical Statistics, vol. 38, 1967, pp. 325–339.

Fishbein, M. and Ajzen, I., Belief, Attitude, Intention and Behavior: An Introduction to Theory and Research. Reading, MA: Addison-Wesley, 1975.

Forbrig, P., "Task and Object-Oriented Development of Interactive Systems – How Many Models are Necessary?," presented at Design Specification and Verification of Interactive Systems Workshop (DSVIS'99), Braga, Portugal, 1999.

Garvin, D. A., "Building a Learning Organization," Harvard Business Review, vol. 71, 1993, pp. 78–91.

Glass, R. A., "A Structure-Based Critique on Contemporary Computing Research," Journal of Systems and Software, vol. 28, 1995, pp. 3–7.

Goldenson, D. R., Gopal, A., and Mukhopadhyay, T., "Determinants of Success in Software Measurement Programs: Initial Results," 153 References presented at Sixth IEEE International Symposium on Software Metrics, Boca Raton, Florida, USA, 1999.

Gorny, P., "EXPOSE – HCI Counseling for User Interface Design," presented at 5th Int'l. Conf. on Human Computer Interaction (Interact '95), Lille-hammer, Norway, 1995.

Gould, J. D. and Lewis, C., "Designing for Usability: Key Principles and What Designers Think," Communications of the ACM, vol. 28, 1985, pp. 360–411.

Grammenos, D., Akoumianakis, D., and Stephanidis, C., "Integrated Support for Working with Guidelines: The Sherlock Guideline Management System," Interacting with Computers, vol. 12, 2000.

Gulliksen, J., Lantz, A., and Boivie, I., "Making User Centred Design Usable," Centre for User Oriented IT Design, Stockholm, Sweden TRITA-NA-D0006, CID-72, 1999.

Hayne, C., Seffah, A., and Engelberg, D., "Comparing Use Cases and Task Analysis: A Concrete Example," in Object-Oriented Technology, ECOOP'99 Workshop Reader, vol. 1743, Lecture Notes in Computer Science, A. M. D. Moreira and S. Demeyer, Eds. Springer, 1999, pp. 248–249.

Henninger, S., "A Methodology and Tools for Applying Context-Specific Usability Guidelines to Interface Design," Interacting with Computers, vol. 12, 2000, pp. 225–243.

Hix, D. and Hartson, H. R., Developing User Interfaces: Ensuring Usability Through Product & Process. New York: John Wiley & Sons, 1993.

Houdek, F., Empirisch basierte Qualitätsverbesserung: Systematischer Einsatz externer Experimente im Software Engineering. Berlin: Logos-Verlag, 1999.

Huber, "Organizational Learning: The Contributing Processes and the Literature," in Organizational Learning, M. D. Cohen and L. S. Sproull, Eds. Sage Publications, 1995.

Hughes, R. T., "Expert Judgement as an Estimating Method," Information and Software Technology, vol. 38, 1996, pp. 67–75.

Humphrey, W. S., Managing the Software Process. Reading: Addison Wesley, 1990. 154 References.

IEEE Std.610.12, "IEEE Standard Glossary of Software Engineering Terminology," in IEEE Standards Collection Software Engineering. New York: The Institute of Electrical and Electronics Engineers (IEEE), 1990, pp. 7–83.

International Organization for Standardization, " ISO/TR Technical Report 18529: Human-Centred Lifecycle Process Descriptions," International Organization for Standardization (ISO), Genève, Switzerland 2000.

ISO/IEC 9126-1, "Software Engineering – Product Quality – Part 1: Quality Model," International Organization for Standardization (ISO) 2001.

ISO-SPICE, "SPICE (ISO/IEC TR 15504-2): Information Technology – Software Process Assessment – Part 2, A Reference Model For Processes and Process Capability," International Organization for Standardization (ISO) 1998.

ISO/TC 159 Ergonomics, "ISO9241- Ergonomic Requirements for Office Work with Visual Display Terminals – Part 11: Guidance on usability," International Organization for Standardization (ISO) ISO 9241-11:1998(E), 1998.

ISO/TC 159 Ergonomics, "ISO 13407:1999(E): Human-Centered Design Processes for Interactive Systems," International Organization for Standardization (ISO) ISO 13407:1999(E), 1999.

Jarke, M., "Scenarios for Modeling," Communications of the ACM, vol. 42, 1999.

John, B. E. and Kieras, D. E.,"Using GOMS for User Interface Design and Evaluation: Which Technique?" ACM Transactions on Computer-Human Interaction, vol. 3, 1996, pp. 287–319.

Judd, C. M., Smith, E. R., and Kidder, L. H., Research Methods in Social Relations, 6th ed., Harcourt Brace Jovanovich College Publishers, 1991.

Juristo, N. and Moreno, A. M., Basics of Software Engineering Experimentation. Dordrecht: Kluwer Academic Publishers, 2001. 155 References.

Kaufmann, A., Introduction to the Theory of Fuzzy Sets. New York: Academic Press, 1975.

Kazman, R., Bass, L., and Bosch, J., "Workshop on Bridging the Gaps Between Software Engineering and Human-Computer Interaction," presented at 25th International Conference on Software Engineering, 2003.

Kickert, W. J. M., Fuzzy Theories on Decision-Making, vol. 3. Leiden, Boston, London: Martinus Nijhoff Social Sciences Division, 1978.

Kirakowski, J. and Corbett, M., "SUMI: The Software Usability Measurement Inventory," British Journal of Educational Technology, vol. 24, No. 3, 1993. pp. 210–212.

Kitchenham, B. A., "Evaluating Software Engineering Methods and Tools, Part1: The Evaluation Context and Methods," ACM SIGSoft Software Engineering Notes, vol. 21, 1996, pp. 11–14.

Kolski, C. and Loslever, P., "An HCI-Enriched Model for Supporting Human-Machine Systems Design and Evaluation," presented at IFAC- Man Machine Systems Conference, Kyoto, Japan, 1998.

Köppen N, W. H. I., "Developing a Process Model for the Design of Assistance Componenets in Information Appliances," presented at 8th IFAC/IFIP/IFORS/IEA Symposium on Anlysis, Design, and Evaluation of Human-Machine Systems. Düsseldorf, 2002.

Krutchen, P., "Use Case Storyboards in the Rational Unified Process (Workshop on Integrating Human Factors in Use Case and OO Methods)," presented at 12th European Conference on Object-Oriented Programming, 1999.

Kuhn, T.S. The Structure of Scientific Revolutions, 1st. ed., Chicago: University of Chicago Press, 1962, p. 168.

Laitenberger, O. and Dreyer, H. M., "Evaluating the Usefulness and the Ease of Use of a Web-based Inspection Data Collection Tool," presented at Fifth IEEE International Symposium on Software Metrics, Bethesda, Maryland, USA, 1998.

Landauer, T. K., The Trouble with Computers: Usefulness, Usability and Productivity: MIT Press, 1995. 156 References.

Lewis, C. and Rieman, J., "Task-Centred User Interface Design," http://www.hcibib.org/tcuid/appx-m.html, 2001.

Lim, K. Y. and Long, J. B., The Muse Method for Usability Engineering, Cambridge University Press, 1994.

Lindley, D. V., Making Decisions. Chichester, UK: John Wiley & Sons, 1975.

Lofland, J. and Lofland, L. H., Analyzing Social Settings: A Guide to Qualitative Observation and Analysis, 3rd ed., Belmont, CA: Wadsworth Publishing Co., 1995.

Lonczewski, F. and Schreiber, S., "The FUSE-System: An Integrated User Interface Design Environment," presented at 2nd International Conference on Computer-Aided Design of User Interfaces (CADUI'96), Namur, France, 1996.

Macleod, M., Bowden, R., Bevan, N., and Curson I., "The MUSiC Performance Measurement Method (PDF, 133K)," Behaviour and Information Technology, vol. 16, 1997.

Macleod, M. and Rengger, R., "The Development of DRUM: A Software Tool for Videoassisted Usability Evaluation," presented at BCS Conference on People and Computers VIII HCI'93, Lougborough, 1993.

Mao, J. and Vredenburg, K., "User-Centered Design Methods in Practice: A Survey of the State of the Art," presented at 11th Annual IBM Centers for Advanced Studies Conference, Toronto, Ontario, Canada, 2001.

Markopoulos, P. and Marijnissen, P., "UML as a Representation for Interaction Designs," presented at Australian Conference on Computer-Human Interaction (OZCHI 2000), 2000.

Mayhew, D. J., The Usability Engineering Lifecycle: A Practioner's Handbook for User Interface Design, Morgan Kaufman Publishers, 1999.

McCall, J., Richards, P., and Walters, G., "Factors in Software Quality," three volumes, NTIS AD-A049-014, AD-A049-015, AD-A049-055, November 1977.

McGill, M. E., Slocum, J. W. J., and Lei, D. T., "Management Practices in Learning Organizations," Organizational Dynamics, vol. 21, 1992, pp. 5–17. 157 References.

McGraw, K. L. and Harbison, K., User-Centered Requirements: The Scenario-Based Engineering Process. Mahwah, NJ: Lawrence Erbaum Associates, 1997.

Melody, Y., Ivory, M. A. Hearst: The State of the Art in Automating Usability Evaluation of User Interfaces. ACM Computing. Survey. vol. 33, No. 4, 2001, 470–516.

Metzker, E., "Evidence-Based Usability Engineering: Seven Thesis on the Integration, Establishment and Continuous Improvement of Human-Centred Design Methods in Software Development Processes," presented at 8th IFIP TC.13 International Coference on Human-Computer Interaction, INTERACT 2001 – Workshop on Cross Pollination Between Software Engineering and Usability Engineering, Tokyo, Japan, 2001a.

Metzker, E., "Supporting Organizational Learning in Usability Engineering," presented at 9th International Conference on Human Computer Interaction, HCI International 2001, New Orleans, LA, USA, 2001b.

Metzker, E. and Offergeld, M., "An Interdisciplinary Approach for Successfully Integrating Human-Centered Design Methods Into Development Processes Practiced by Industrial

Software Development Organizations," in Engineering for Human Computer Interaction: 8th IFIP International Conference, EHCI 2001(EHCI'01), Lecture Notes in Computer Science, R. Little and L. Nigay, Eds. Toronto, Canada: Springer, 2001a, pp. 21–36.

Metzker, E. and Offergeld, M., "REUSE: Computer-Aided Improvement of Human-Centered Design Processes," presented at Mensch und Computer, 1st Interdisciplinary Conference of the German Chapter of the ACM, Bad Honnef, Germany, 2001b.

Metzker, E. and Offergeld, M., "Success Factors for the Introduction, Establishment and Continuous Improvement of Human-Centered Design Processes in Industrial Software Development Projects," presented at 6th Congress on Software Quality Management, SQM 2001, Bonn, Germany, 2001c.

Metzker, E. and Reiterer, H., "Evidence-Based Usability Engineering," presented at Computer-aided Design of User Interfaces (CADUI2002), Valenciennes, France, 2002a.

Metzker, E. and Reiterer, H., "Use and Reuse of HCI Knowledge in the Software Development Lifecycle: Existing Approaches and What Developers Think," in Usability – Gaining a Competitive Edge, J. Hammond, T. Gross, and J. Wesson, Eds. Norwell, Massachusetts: Kluwer Academic Publishers, 2002b, pp. 39–55.

Moore, G. and Benbasat, I., "Development of an Instrument to Measure the Perceptions of Adopting an Information Technology Innovation," Information Systems Research, vol. 2, 1991, pp. 192–222.

Myers, B. A., "User Interface Software Tools," ACM Transactions on Computer-Human Interaction, vol. 2, 1995, pp. 64–108.

Nielsen, J., "Heuristic Evaluation," in Usability Inspection Methods, J. Nielsen and R. L. Mack, Eds. New York: Wiley, 1994a.

Nielsen, J., Usability Engineering: Morgan Kaufman Publishers, 1994b.

Niessink, F. and Van Vliet, H., "Measurements Should Generate Value, Rather than Data," presented at 6th IEEE International Symposium on Software Metrics, Boca Raton, Florida, USA, 1999.

Norman, D. A., The Invisible Computer: MIT Press, 1998.

Nunes, N. J. and Cunha, J. F., "Wisdom: A Software Engineering Method for Small Softwaredevelopment Companies. Software," IEEE, vol. 17, No. 5, Sep/Oct 2000, pp. 113–119.

Nunnally, J. C., and Bernstein, I. H., Psychometric Theory, 3rd ed., New York: McGraw-Hill, 1994.

Oed, R., Becker, A., and Wetzenstein, E., "Welche Unterstützung wünschen Softwareentwickler beim Entwurf von Bedienoberflächen," presented at Mensch & Computer 2001, Bad Honnef, 2001.

Owen, E., Agerfalk, P., "Information Modeling Based on a Meaningful Use of Language," CAiSE Workshops, vol. 1, 2004, pp. 249–262.

Paterno, F., "Towards a UML for Interactive Systems," presented at Engineering for Human-Computer-Interaction (EHCI2001), Toronto, Canada, 2001.

Paterno, F., "Commentary on 'Scenarios and Task Analysis' by Dan Diaper," Interacting with Computers, vol. 14, 2002, pp. 407–409.

Perry, D. E., Porter, A. A., and Votta, L. G., "Empirical Studies of Software Engineering: A Roadmap," presented at International Conference on Software Engineering (ICSE2000), Limerick, Ireland, 2000.

Pinheiro da Silva, P. and Paton, N.W., "A UML-Based Design Environment for Interactive Applications," presented at UIDIS'01, Zurich, Switzerland, 2001.

Polson, P. G., Lewis, C. H., Rieman, J., and Wharton, C., "Cognitive Walkthroughs: A Method for Theory-Based Evaluation of User Interfaces," International Journal of Man-Machine Studies, vol. 36, 1992, pp. 741–773.

Preece, J., Rogers, Y., et al. Human-Computer Interaction, Addison-Wesley, 1994.

Pressman, R. S., Software Engineering: A Practitioner's Approach. New York: McGraw Hill, 1992.

Puerta, A. R. and Maulsby, D., "MOBI-D: A Model-Based Development Environment for User Centered Design," presented at Human Factors in Computer Science (CHI), Atlanta, USA, 1997.

Reed, P., Holdaway, K., Isensee, S., Buie, E., Fox, J., Williams, J., and Lund, A., "User Interface Guidelines and Standards: Progress, Issues and Prospects," Interacting with Computers, vol. 12, 1999.

Reiterer, H., "Tools for Working with Guidelines in Different User Interface Design Approaches," presented at Annual Workshop of the Special Interest Group on Tools for Working with Guidelines, Biarritz, France, 2000.

Riemenschneider, C. K., Hardgrave, B. C., and Davis, F. D., "Explaining Developer Acceptance of Formal Software Methodologies: An Integration of Five Theoretical Models," University of Arkansas, Information Technology Research Center # ITRC-WP011-0900, 2000.

Roberts, D., Designing for the User with OVID: Bridging User Interface Design and Software Engineering. Indianapolis, USA: Macmillan Technical Publishing, 1998, 189p. ISBN: 1578701015.

Robey, D., "Research Commentary: Diversity in Information Systems Research: Threat, Promise and Responsibility," Information Systems Reserach, vol. 7, 1996, pp. 400–408. 160 References.

Rosenbaum, S., Chauncey, E. W., Jokela, T., Rohn, J. A., Smith, T. B., and Vredenburg, K., "Usability in Practice: User Experience Lifecycle – Evolution and Revolution," presented at CHI 2002, Minneapolis, Minnesota, USA, 2002.

Rosenbaum, S., Rohn, J. A., and Humburg, J., "A Toolkit for Startegic Usability: Results from Workshops, Panels and Surveys," presented at Conference on Human Factors in Computing Systems (CHI'00), The Hague, Netherlands, 2000.

Rosenberg, L. and Hyatt, L., "Developing a Successful Metrics Program," presented at 8th Annual Software Technology Conference, Utah, USA, 1996.

Rosson, M. B., "Integrating Development of Task and Object Models," Communication of the ACM, vol. 42, 1999, pp. 49–56.

Rosson, M. B., Carroll, J. M., Cerra, D. D., and Hill, N., Usability Engineering: Scenario-Based Development of Human Computer Interaction: Morgan Kaufmann, 2001.

Schneiderman, B., "Designing the User Interface: Strategies for Effective Human-computer Interaction, Addison-Wesley, 1992, pp. 573.

Scholtz, j., Laskowski, D., "Developing Usability Tools and Techniques for Designing and Testing Web Site," Proceedings of the 4th Conference on Human Factors and the Web, 1998.

Sears, A., "AIDE: A Step Toward Metric-Based Interface Development Tools," in Proceedings of the 8th ACM Symposium on User Interface Software and Technology, Pittsburgh, PA, USA. ACM, pp. 101–110, 1995.

Seffah, A. and Hayne, C., "Integrating Human Factors in Use Case and OO Methods," presented at 12th European Conference on Object-Oriented Programming, Lisbon, Portugal, 1999.

Seffah, A. and Metzker, E., "The Obstacles and Myths of Usability and Software Engineering," Communications of the ACM, vol. 47, 2004.

Shackel, B., "Usability – Context, Framework, Design and Evaluation," in Human Factors for Informatics Usability, B. Shackel, and S. Richardson, eds., Cambridge: Cambridge University Press, 1991, pp. 21–28.

Shafer, G., A Mathematical Theory of Evidence, Princton, NJ: Princton University Press, 1976.

Sheppard, B. H., Hartwick, J., and Warshaw, P. R., "The Theory of Reasoned Action: A Meta-Analysis of Past Research with Recommendations for Modifications and Future Research," Journal of Consumer Research, vol. 15, 1988, pp. 325–343.

Shewart, W. A., Economic Control of Quality of Manufactured Product, New York: D. Van Nostrand Company Inc., 1931.

Shrivastava, P. and Mitroff, I. I., "Enhancing Organizational Research Utilization: The Role of Decision Makers' Assumptions," Academy of Management Review, vol. 9, 1984, pp. 18–26.

Silverman, B. G., "Software Cost and Productivity Improvements: An Analogical View," IEEE Computer, vol. 18, 1985, pp. 86–96.

Simon, H. A., The Sciences of the Artificial, 2nd ed., Cambridge, MA: MIT Press, 1981.

Smith, A. and Dunckley, L., "User Centred Design: The Application of the LUCID Interface Design Method," presented at HCI International, 1997.

Smith, G. F. and March, S. T., "Design and Natural Science Research on Information Technology," Decision Support Systems, vol. 15, 1995, pp. 251–266.

Smith, S. L. and Mosier, J. N., "Guidelines for Designing User Interface Software," The MITRE Coporation, Bedford ESD-TR-86 278 MTR-10090, 1986.

Spencer, R., "The Streamlined Cognitive Walkthrough Method: Working Around Social Constraints Encountered in a Software Development Company," presented at Conference on Human Factors in Computing Systems (CHI'00), The Hague, 2000.

Stapleton, J., DSDM, Dynamic Systems Development Method: The Method in Practice: Addison Wesley Professional, 1997.

Stirewalt, K., Davila, D., Rugaber, S., and Browne, T., "The MASTERMIND User-interface Generation Project," in Applications of Formal Methods in Human-Computer Interaction, Springer, 1997.

Sutcliffe, A., "On the Effective Use and Reuse of HCI Knowledge," ACM Transactions on Computer-Human Interaction, vol. 7, 2001, pp. 197–221.

Tetzlaff, L. and Schwartz, D. R., "The Use of Guidelines in Interface Design," presented at ACM Conference on Human Factors in Computing Systems (CHI '91), New Orleans, 1991.

Tidwell, J., "Common Ground: A Pattern Language for Human-Computer Interface Design," 1999. http://www.mit.edu/~jtidwell/interaction_patterns.html.

Thimbleby, H., "On Discerning Users," in How to Make User-Centred Design Usable, J. Gulliksen, A. Lantz, and I. Boivie, Eds., Stockholm: Royal Institute of Technology Stockholm – Center for User Oriented IT Design (CID), 2000, pp. 63–85.

Triantaphyllou, E., Multi-Criteria Decision Making Methods – A Comparative Study. Dordrecht, The Netherlands: Kluwer Academic Publishers, 2000.

Vanderdonckt, J., "Development Milestones Towards a Tool for Working with Guidelines," Interacting with Computers, vol. 12, 1999, pp. 81–118.

Vredenburg, K. and Butler, M. B., "Current Practice and Future Directions in User-Centred Design," presented at 5th Annual Conference of the Usability Professionals Association, Copper Mountain, Colorado, USA, 1996.

Weinschenk, S. and Yeo, S. C., Guidelines for Enterprise-Wide GUI design, New York: Wiley, 1995.

Welie, M. v., "Breaking Down Usability," presented at IFIP TC.13 International Conference on Human-Computer Interaction (INTERACT), Endinburgh, UK, 1999.

Zadeh, L., "Fuzzy Sets," Information and Control, vol. 8, No. 3, pp. 338–353, 1965.

Zelkowitz, M. V., "Modeling Software Engineering Environment Capabilities," Journal of Systems and Software, vol. 35, No. 1, pp. 3–14, 1996.

Zelkowitz, M. V. and Wallace, D. R. "Experimental Models for Validating Technology," IEEE Computer, vol. 31, No. 5, pp. 23–31, 1998.

Index